bare feet

By

Debbie Ali

Printed Book ISBN: 9798795923154

Publisher: Debbie Ashmeed-Ali

Editor-in-chief: Beth McBlain

Book Design and Layout: Ansara Ali and Eddie Chan

Cover Design: Ansara Ali – ansaraali2@gmail.com

This book is dedicated to all humanity.

PSALM 23

The Lord is my shepherd; I shall not want.

He maketh me to lie down in green pastures; He leadeth me beside the still waters.

He restoreth my soul: He leadeth me in the paths of righteousness for His name's sake.

Yea, though I walk through the valley of the shadow of death, I will fear no evil: for thou art with me; thy rod and thy staff they comfort me.

Thou preparest a table before me in the presence of mine enemies: thou anointest my head with oil; my cup runneth over.

Surely goodness and mercy shall follow me all the days of my life: and I will dwell in the house of the LORD forever.

AMEN.

ACKNOWLEDGEMENTS

The sole reason that I am alive, have survived and continue to thrive in this lifetime is due to my Lord and Saviour Jesus Christ. He has been my rock and my place of refuge from early childhood. He is my greatest source of comfort. There are no words to express the depth of my connection with the Almighty and still I know that I know nothing.

To my children, I say an endless thank you for tolerating my many moods and the roller coaster ride that our lives have been at certain times. Know that your 24/7 support and love have helped me keep my head above water in times when death by drowning was a near certainty.

To my mother, who has always been my rock. It is your faith and strength that have rubbed off on me and this I can never repay.

To my husband, words cannot do justice to my feelings for you. You have always been my warmth, my place of security – you are home to me.

To the newest member of my tribe, Beth McBlain, you have not only been my Editor and guide throughout this revamping process, but you have been my friend. Beth, your endless positivity and light have kept me on course and pointed me in the direction of digging even deeper within myself. For this, I am eternally grateful.

Finally, I wish to thank everyone who has supported my endeavours over the years, especially my passion for helping others.

This company includes very close family members, friends who are like my blood relatives, and even those perfect strangers who have become my spiritual family.

Bare Feet has been a divine calling but I would never have completed this task without the support of my entire family and the very few I consider to be close friends. You know who you are. To you all words have not been invented to express my gratitude and love.

ABOUT THE AUTHOR

 Debbie Ali was born and raised on a tropical island in the Caribbean known as Trinidad and Tobago. It was there she honed her skills as both a professional writer and teacher. Currently she resides in Canada and is the founder of 3GL Consulting. This company is very personal to her as her vision is to create 'safe spaces' for everyone. Debbie has assisted many individuals to create physical, mental, emotional and spiritual safe spaces for themselves, thus allowing those individuals to develop in life, find peace and healing and to achieve personal goals.

As a Consultant, Coach and Counsellor Debbie Ali has been the recipient of a Lifetime Achievement Award for her tireless work in addressing issues such as PTSD, anxiety, depression, suicide, and self-esteem issues, among a host of others. She has always been a strong advocate for women's rights with great emphasis placed on curbing violence against women.

A prolific public speaker Debbie has spread her message of forgiveness, peace, love and hope on many platforms. In addition, she has worked with adolescents and adults of varying ages, cultures, religions and ethnicities to find healing and peace. The skills and techniques she teaches deeply resonate with individuals because she can personally relate to the trauma they have endured.

Furthermore, she has used the techniques she teaches in her own life as a source of personal healing. They are practical, easy to employ in everyday life and very effective. Debbie builds relationships with everyone she works with and her follow-up and genuine concern makes a powerful difference to those who are still struggling.

Debbie's experience as a teacher, tutor, mentor, writer, manager and her extensive work in the areas of public relations and mass communications have allowed her a holistic view of people and the psychology behind their thinking. For a time she hosted her own radio program. She is a frequent guest on all forms of media. She attributes all of her blessings to God and insists that her greatest blessings are her two imperfect children.

TABLE OF CONTENTS

FOOTPRINTS IN THE SAND

One night a man had a dream. He dreamed he was walking
along the beach with the LORD.
Across the sky flashed scenes from his life.
For each scene he noticed two sets of
footprints in the sand: one belonging
to him, and the other to the LORD.
When the last scene of his life flashed before him,
he looked back at the footprints in the sand.
He noticed that many times along the path of
his life there was only one set of footprints.
He also noticed that it happened at the very
lowest and saddest times in his life.
This really bothered him and he
questioned the LORD about it:
"LORD, you said that once I decided to follow
you, you'd walk with me all the way.
But I have noticed that during the most
troublesome times in my life,
there is only one set of footprints.
I don't understand why when
I needed you most, you would leave me."
The LORD replied:
"My son, my precious child,
I love you and I would never leave you.
During your times of trial and suffering,
when you see only one set of footprints,
it was then that I carried you."

Author: Carolyn Joyce Carty

CHAPTER 1
Introduction, Why I wrote Bare Feet ...

Welcome Reader, my name is Debbie Ali. In 2006, at the age of 31, I was kidnapped from my home in Trinidad and held for ransom for fourteen days and nights. During my captivity I was badly beaten, starved, dehydrated, kept in chains and raped multiple times. By the time of my release I was presumed dead by the police, and indeed the entire nation.

My kidnapping does not appear to have been personal; we were not wealthy, nor do I suggest it was politically motivated as no one in our family was a public figure. To the best of my knowledge, I was taken in a random criminal act, quite simply a crime of opportunity. The kidnappers stationed themselves in my then community, spent time observing our simple lifestyle and our daily routines and then reached into my life, my world, my home and plucked me out of everything that was safe and familiar to me.

As a wife and mother I had led a very sheltered life, surrounded by my family living in an ordinary middle class community. My abduction changed my life, my dreams, my goals and my perceptions forever. It also changed the lives of my nearest and dearest, even the lives of my extended family members. How could any of us ever be the same again? It was a horrendous experience. I survived because of my faith in God and my determined, dedicated focus on getting back to my two darling children.

Before this experience, I was definitely a slightly naïve idealistic young woman. I believed in love at first sight and anticipated being cherished, worshiped and revered as my husband's ideal woman. He would be my 'Prince Charming', and together we would build a picture-perfect life, creating a cozy little family and living happily ever after. Those dreams were, of course, girlish fantasies; ultimately, I did manage to realize some of those daydreams and visions while other considerations remain totally out of reach for me and my family, even today.

My reason for writing this book and sharing my experiences is that I hope, by shining a light on my hard-won understanding, I can be of service to others. Perhaps the lessons I have learned can prevent you, Dear Reader, from ever living through a similar horrific experience. Or, if something like this ever does happen to you, then perhaps my experiences might provide you with at least some basic information, strategies, thoughts and plans about how to survive.

As you read on I urge you to examine your life. I encourage you to contemplate your home, your routines, your neighbourhood, and to consider the lessons I have learned about preparing and creating a safe environment. You cannot prevent catastrophe but you can do more to keep yourself and your family safe and more secure.

In these pages I will attempt to teach you to become much more mindful and conscious of your routines, your immediate surroundings and general environment. This is the key to creating all safe spaces, be they physical, mental, emotional or even spiritual.

If you have already suffered terrible abuse, kidnapping or exploitation, please let me take this time to offer my condolences and also congratulations to you and your family. You are a survivor just like me.

Perhaps reading my story will bring you some peace with the realization that you are not alone. You are not the only one who has gone through this horrible and life-changing experience.

Abductions, abuse, kidnapping and human trafficking are difficult topics, and not often discussed in the media, yet statistics indicate that these horrific events happen somewhere close to you each and every day.

The statistics are almost incomprehensible. According to the United Nations one of the leading global concerns is violence against women in all its forms. Do the math, if 1 in 3 women have experienced some manner of violence or sexual assault in their lifetimes, what must be the number of lives that have been touched by this pain in every city, every country. Further consider that these statistics are based on crimes that were actually reported. Estimates are that perhaps only 1 in 10 cases of sexual assault are actually reported.

As if it could get no worse, over 50% of these violent acts committed are against girls under the age of 16. And what of the women who are beaten by their partners being 48% more likely to contract HIV/AIDS? What of those lives?

Over 2.5 million people are trafficked annually around the world and women account for 80% of those victims.

I urge you, do not only look at the numbers, but remember each number represents so many individuals - women, young girls, human beings - lives that have been endangered and scarred forever.

Scarred as in changed forever, because beyond survival there comes recovery. Inevitably there are physical, mental and emotional consequences that arise after enduring any type of abuse, violence or trauma.

These consequences reach beyond the individual, encom-passing their friends and family and most especially their children.

I have struggled with nervousness, anxiety and paranoia about my personal safety and the safety of my family since being released by my captors. I have been hyper focused on ways to create a safe environment for myself and my family members every day of my life. This book is the result of those experiences.

Thankfully, slowly but gradually I have also re-learned how to allow myself to experience some joy in this world. The harsh reality is that when certain things are taken away from you, your life can NEVER fully return to the way that it was, but it CAN get better.

My grounding factors were, and continue to be, the angelic faces of my two children. They remind me of the person I am meant to be. Sometimes, however, even that is not enough to curb the bouts of depression and isolation. This book is my way of reclaiming my own power. These days I choose to see myself not just as a survivor but as someone who is thriving in this life despite my setbacks. Much of what you will read in the following pages are the words and messages that came to me during my abduction. My faith in God gave me the strength to survive; these revelations came to me in the form of visions, audible messages from God, and my death experience. I have healed since then and learnt many heart wrenching lessons along the way but I had the will and Jesus Christ made the way.

CLIPS FROM THE PAST

Kidnap victim: I saw Jesus

Sat Jan 02 2010

While being held captive by kidnappers, she felt like she died, went to heaven, and saw Jesus. "I felt my life leaving me, but at no point did I cease to be who I am. I was taken to a place where there was rest, release, peace. "Nothing like pain there; no fear, no anxiety. Sadness and grief? It was impossible to feel those things. "I tried to feel sad about leaving my children, but I couldn't," kidnap survivor, Debbie Ali, told the Sunday Guardian last week. Ali said she must have been "dead" for about two hours, because she felt her life leave her around midday and her breath return in the early afternoon.

Kidnapped on December 5, 2006, from her Roystonia, Couva home, she reveals an astounding spiritual encounter she had during her two weeks of captivity in her soon-to-be-released book, "Bare Feet." A former teacher who now describes herself as a writer, Ali has two children with her pilot husband. Although by no means wealthy, Ali was abducted and brutalised for ransom, news reports at the time stated. She says she was "mandated" by God to write the book and tell of her spiritual experience. She says she even heard God speaking to her in an audible voice, telling her how to market the book. "He told me to go to Oprah Winfrey and Obama with the book." This may sound far-fetched to some, but Ali says she is now "only a phone call away" from making this a reality. "A lot of people will think I'm a nut case and will not believe me; but that doesn't change the fact that the experience exists."

Chained, raped, tortured

She was chained to a bed with a dog chain, raped and, "tortured more than any woman could bear," slapped, choked, kicked and cuffed.

"I had a pit bull maul me two, three nights. I had to keep dodging it, but it managed to bite out pieces of my hair. "I was blindfolded and didn't see light for 14 days. I got eye and ear infections because of the sweat and tears. My vision has never been the same. "I was thrown into a hole in the ground and kept there for one day. Ali tells all in raw, frank style in "Bare Feet," which was a torment to write, she said. "It was reliving the entire thing again. I would write one line and be sick for weeks. "It was not a healing process. Had it not been mandated to me to write this book, I would have never written it. "I had to tell of the spiritual experience I had while in captivity.

I felt my life pass away and leave my body. I've been to Heaven."

It wasn't just a state of mind she was in, either. "I saw, touched, tasted and felt," Ali said. "I saw Jesus." Asked to describe Him, she said after a pause, "He was like light and spirit with a human silhouette. "He lifted me and held me in His arms and nothing is comparable to that experience. "God wants me to write about the experience to show that He exists and He knows, sees and hears all that is done in darkness and in light; and that He saves. "The kidnapping was only a vehicle to expose this experience." Her spiritual encounter is what gives her the will to live. "This experience I had in Heaven is what keeps me going. If I don't relive it, I can't get through the day. It reminds me of where I'm going," Ali said nothing in the world had any meaning to her any more, including material possessions.

Despite her heavenly encounter, Ali feels she has been permanently damaged by what the kidnappers did to her. "I don't feel vindicated, in terms of justice being served. I heard through the grapevine that my case is not on the files; that it was closed because there is no evidence." While Ali's ordeal does not exist in the police files, it remains a nightmare that haunts her daily. "The experience goes into my family, my kids, my marriage, with long-term effects. "I don't think I'll ever be whole again. You really just can't, after such an experience." After three years, it has become easier to bear. But time had only eased the impact, Ali said. "I still take pills to go to sleep. I still have nightmares and wake up cold-sweating." Ali sought the help of top T&T psychologists, but found none trained to deal with survivors of crime. She tried to set up a support group for female crime survivors, but had difficulty accessing funding. "I try to talk to women. The Anti-Kidnapping Unit used to refer women victims of crime to me."

Ali case still open

Sat Jan 09 2010

The Debbie Ali kidnapping case is far from closed and the matter is still under investigation, Deputy Police Commissioner Gilbert Reyes disclosed last Wednesday. Reyes, responding to questions from the Sunday Guardian about the reported closure of the case, said, "The case is not closed. It is still open. The police are still doing investigations. In fact, we are working on some leads in the matter at this time."

Reyes admitted that the police sometimes do not do "follow-up" work in informing crime survivors on how their matters are proceeding and assured, "I am going to call the Anti-Kidnapping Unit (AKU) and have them go to Ali and update her on the case." Ali was kidnapped from her Roystonia, Couva home, on December 5, 2006, and to date, no one has been held in connection with the crime. Reyes commended Ali for "being a very brave lady" and said her speaking out openly about her ordeal has given the police help.

Police Tackle Kidnapping Surge in Trinidad

Debbie Ali became one of the scourge's victims late last year as she was cleaning the gutters outside her house one morning shortly before Christmas. She says she was aware that there were plenty of people out, potentially witnesses, when she started cleaning. When the outside traffic began to thin, she prepared to go back inside, knowing it was unsafe to be alone and that she was a prime target for a kidnapping. Then the phone rang, and she ran inside to get it.

"I picked up the phone. I had my keys in my hand," she describes. "I was just moving to hit the button for the garage door to close and just as I turned around, these two men came in ... masked."

Ali lives about an hour outside Port of Spain in an upper-middle-class neighborhood of two-story stucco houses, two-car garages and manicured lawns. It looks more like a suburb of Houston than an area right outside of Port of Spain.

Ali, who stands at just 5 feet tall and weighs about 80 pounds, says that when she saw the men behind her, she couldn't move.

"Your reaction is not snap, to run inside and lock the door, whatever," she says. "You just freeze — and that is sheer shock and sheer terror. You literally go cold. I felt like I had no blood in my body."

At first, Ali was hoping that it would just be a robbery, that the men would ransack the house, take jewelry and money, and then leave. But when they started to look for things to tie her up, she realized that it was going to be much more.

"They came with my husband's ties, and they tied my hands and feet. And they put a pillowcase over my head, and that's when I knew," Ali says.

She knew she was about to be kidnapped.

17

"An abnormal reaction to an abnormal situation is normal behaviour."

- Viktor Frankl

CHAPTER 2
The Taking

This is the official term that refers to the actual kidnapping, the event when you are taken away against your free will.

If there are no opportunities for escape, or if you are injured in a struggle and cannot avoid being led away then there are many issues which you MUST consider, given your dire situation.

YOUR HEALTH
Instinctively, your survival instincts will kick in, causing adrenaline to be pumped and your heart rate to increase substantially. Medical professionals describe this as a normal physical reaction and claim it cannot be curbed except with the use of medication, but these physiological responses will wear you down and can cause extreme exhaustion. You must work to control your body's response. There are techniques that can help.

When I was taken, I drew upon knowledge gleaned from reading (I am an avid reader) and I was able to eventually reduce my heart rate. This enabled me to remain calmer and thus able to think a bit clearer about my situation. It is also important to note that if you are injured and bleeding an elevated heart rate will increase how quickly you are bleeding, further endangering your life. Therefore, reducing or normalizing your heart rate will decrease the speed of blood flow; this could save your life.

If you are injured, then you MUST try to preserve your life at all costs. Ask your captors to clean and bandage your wound(s) to stop any bleeding and prevent infection. Ask in a soft, humble voice. This denotes respect for their position of authority over you (regardless of how angry and scared you are). Before making a request, always ask permission to speak first. This behaviour will make them feel in control of you and the situation. They may be less inclined to be harsh with you, and more willing to accede to your request. Of course, you must 'feel out' your captors.

This is extremely difficult to do and even if you feel that you have them figured out, you could still be wrong and your approach could backfire. In other words, you will be taking a tremendous risk by speaking, however, it is vitally important and the risk may be worth taking, if your survival depends upon it.

If you sense that your kidnappers may possess some compassion, then in my humble estimation, it is okay to lie. In an attempt to gain sympathy (especially if you are a woman) you can say that you are a diabetic, need special medication for allergies, migraines or even your time of the month. These untruths cannot be disputed at that point in time and you MAY receive extra care, especially in moving you around. If injuries, cuts and bruises are avoided, this can preserve your health and your life. This strategy may not work, but then again, it just might. In my case, I told them of my illnesses, which was the truth. The only lie I told was about suspected diabetes!

One must also consider that your kidnappers may choose to verify your complaints with whomever they are negotiating. If they discover you are lying, this will erode any trust between you and them. In my instance, I opted to tell one lie (suspected diabetes) because I realized that my kidnappers were not communicating often with my husband and it was unlikely for them to ask about something so 'trivial' as my health care needs when there were ransom matters to discuss. So again, I weighed my situation and my options and tried under such terrifying conditions to make the best choice possible.

Remember, you can only do what you can to survive the best than you can at that specific moment. You can only do your very best, given your limited knowledge of your captors and their motives.

DO NOT DRAW ATTENTION TO YOURSELF.
Be as quiet as possible; and if you must speak, do so as softly as possible. If you perceive that your kidnapper(s) are rough and possess no compassion, then refrain from speaking as this could result in further injury or death.

Remember, while you can try to appeal to the better nature of these criminals, they are still criminals and most likely do not value you as a person. You and your loved ones mean absolutely nothing to them and your life is very much disposable. You are the only one who wants you to stay alive.

Occasionally kidnappers will hire underhanded doctors to treat their hostages, if it is absolutely necessary; after all, although your kidnappers can likely kill you without batting an eyelash, they also need to keep you alive at least for a little while. For a short time at least, you are a 'package' which can be exchanged for money. Forget your wealth and your social position because when you are abducted it all means absolutely nothing; your circumstances are now primitive with basic survival instincts kicking in to save your own life.

PAY CLOSE ATTENTION TO WHAT IS HAPPENING AROUND YOU.
Note as many details as possible to relay to the police in the event that you do escape or are released.

• Try to note your kidnappers' voices, speech patterns, skin colour, identifying marks such as tattoos or unique facial features, physical characteristics such as eye or hair colour, their mode of dress, even their shoes or cologne. Although the criminals are masked, you can still observe quite a bit using your senses; even a smell or cigarette brand can aid in a police investigation.

• Try as far as possible to make a note of which direction you may be travelling. Look for landmarks, should you have any opportunity to see around you. If not, you can rely on your senses of smell, touch, and hearing. I have learnt that if your sight is removed you can actually learn more about the environment around you than if you were to simply look around. I now have the utmost respect for the visually-impaired persons in our society. I marvel at their abilities. They can teach us 'normal' folk how to truly appreciate our surroundings.

• Try to listen carefully and note the sounds of other people, even children, and what they might be saying. Note the sounds of animals, or specific sounds that occur at regular intervals such as helicopters or airplanes etc. Pay attention to distinctive things – smells like perfume, types of voices and accents, the sounds of weapons.

• If you can try to estimate how long your drive was and even the kinds of roads you travelled on. You can try to assess what kind of vehicle you are travelling in and possibly at what speed. Listen to the engine. Is it a basic engine or a high performance one? What kind of seats are in the vehicle? Leather or fabric. Is the radio on? If so, what station, what kind of music is being played? Do you hear sirens around? Can you estimate what time of day you are at a specific location. Are there lots of potholes in the road? Are you going uphill or downhill? Is the road paved or unpaved? Answers to all of these questions may provide invaluable information for the police to work with.

• If you 'change hands'; that is, if someone else takes charge of you, then remember, that this person's temperament may be very different from the previous person. As such, do not interact with them until you feel that you have a fair idea of their temperament. Of course, speak softly and ask permission to speak first. Always behave in a way that respects and acknowledges the power of the kidnapper.

Strategies for reducing your heart rate

The following are some very specific strategies to reduce the heart rate. It is important to note that these methods worked for me and they may or may not work for you. It is equally essential to remember that it is extremely difficult to engage in these practices for long periods of time. They can be exhausting mentally and emotionally. During my kidnapping I was only able to conduct these exercises successfully for short periods of time but I repeated them as often as I could.

After enduring sheer terror for forty-eight hours non-stop, resulting in a sustained elevated heart rate, my body went into shock sometime on the third day of captivity. I began to convulse uncontrollably, until I passed out. When I regained consciousness, the kidnapper was anxiously slapping me, shaking me and calling me by name. When he realized that I was alive, he checked my pulse and gave me two generic pain-killers for my migraine and some juice. I realized that I had to keep my heart rate under control. I began practicing some techniques I acquired from reading over the years. I succeeded in implementing the following methods from time to time and I strongly believe that they helped to save my life.

Please bear in mind that this is but a mere outline of each strategy and much practice is required to effectively implement each technique.

- Take three deep breaths through your nostrils. Let the air completely fill your lungs to their maximum capacity. Inhale in so deeply that it causes your tummy to extend out. Hold it for a second or two, and then exhale slowly through your mouth. Do this a few times or as often as you feel is needed at the time. Do this slowly and mindfully.

- Mentally envision yourself in your own bed at home, snuggling down to a restful night's sleep. Make yourself smell these familiar scents of your own bed sheets and clothing. Mentally feel your sheets around you on your secure spot on the bed. Do the same breathing exercise as above but this time as you inhale actually smell your sheets.

- Relax your muscles and slowly doze off into restful slumber. This worked somewhat but not often enough.

Another technique:
- Mentally visualize your heart, in your chest rapidly pumping away in anxiety.

- See the arteries, see the blood vessels, see the blood and hear the actual rapid heartbeat.

- Slowly envision the heart slowing its pumping action. This can also be done with the deep breathing exercise. With every heartbeat, hear the beat gradually slowing down until it normalizes.

- Finish the exercise by taking one more slow deep breath and exhale slowly through your nostrils.

By lowering your heart rate you may be able to:
- Avoid going into shock.

- Preserve your physical energy.

- Preserve your nervous energy.

- Give yourself encouragement and a greater sense of control. Your kidnapper controls your fate but you can at least control yourself, if given the opportunity.

- Control sweating and thus conserve your precious body fluids to possibly avoid faster dehydration. This is extremely important.

- Achieve a calmer state of mind, which will facilitate clearer thinking and better decision-making. These methods can also be used during your day-to-day life as a way to relieve stress and anxiety attacks. It works and I am living proof.

Even after the negotiating process has begun, you must face the reality that you will probably have to remain in captivity, at least for a while.

In my case, after day one, I knew that I was in for the long haul. Of course, every minute you spend bound and gagged, masked and chained feels like an eternity, but you must prepare yourself to accept that this might go on for days or even weeks.

The crime of kidnapping humiliates, defiles, and mutilates one's spirit almost beyond recognition. A kidnapper is with- holding another person's right to use the washroom when needed, the right to privacy, the right to scratch an itch, the right to breathe, to speak, to ask for necessities; their very right to exist. This is inhumane and monstrous in nature.

No one should have the authority to stop someone else from seeing their own family, from entertaining themselves, to prevent them from seeing God's creations let alone breathing fresh air. I have forcibly discovered that if one can live alone, with one's self, then one truly has peace. Sometimes, the most difficult person to live with is you. It is at these times that you come face to face with your worst fears, doubts, traumas and needs. One of the worst fears we, as human beings, harbour is the fear of living and dying alone.

I've got news for the human race. While we live among people and thrive on social relationships, we are ALWAYS alone within ourselves. People often become depressed when they discover this loneliness within. This can only be overcome with a deep, strong relationship with the divine being – God Almighty, whomever we see him as.

Lessons Learned

• Manage your health. You cannot take advantage of an unexpected opportunity to escape, or perhaps even survive this experience if you do not take care of your physical and mental well-being. Make it a priority long before it might be necessary.

• Always pay attention to what's happening around you. Those details can make a difference when the police are trying to investigate your case when you emerge from the other end of this experience.

• Make an effort to learn the breathing techniques mentioned. They will serve you well during times of stress that have nothing to do with being kidnapped.

• We are born into this world alone (not in the spiritual sense); we make our choices and decisions alone and we will face the consequences alone as well. But one never feels so isolated, as when one is kidnapped; when there is nothing and no one familiar in our environment. The burning question arises, "*What do I do with myself? I cannot move, speak, watch television, listen to music, take a walk, use the phone or bathroom, and to top it off, I am so terrified that I will be killed or tortured or raped?*"

• I have no solution to offer but my own, and what worked for me in my darkest hours may not work for you; I offer it to you as a real possibility. If it helps to spare just one person my agony, then this book will have served its purpose.

*"Hope is necessary in every condition.
The miseries of poverty, sickness and captivity
would, without this comfort, be insupportable."*

- William Samuel Johnson

CHAPTER 3
Captivity

'**Captive**' – taken prisoner, in confinement; unable to escape. (Oxford Dictionary Definition)

'**Torture**' – infliction of severe bodily pain; severe physical or mental pain; to distort, strain or wrench. (Oxford Dictionary Definition)

These are words that come to mind when one considers the rigors of being held hostage. Yet, they are grossly inadequate for describing the horrors of enduring captivity. It all began on the morning of my 31st birthday, on December 5th 2006. I was occupied doing what any wife and mother would be doing during the run up to Christmas celebrations. It was my favourite time of the year and although that fateful Tuesday should have been a time to relax, I preferred to spend it cleaning for a surprise party I was planning for my beloved husband. That afternoon, I was supposed to see both my kids perform at a Christmas concert at their primary school. My beautiful daughter was supposed to do her very first dance routine and my darling son, his first musical piece. Their intention was for me to be so very surprised! Off they went with their daddy to buy me birthday presents while I remained at home; alone.

Oftentimes it is when we are most relaxed and secure that disaster strikes. I hadn't an inkling of what was lurking just around the corner of my home, my haven, my little family's nest. It is noteworthy to say that although I was in a generally jovial mood, I was not complacent to the point where I was overly careless. I monitored what was taking place in the outdoor environment. There were neighbours milling around and water trucks conducting some maintenance work on pipelines on our street. Thus I felt relatively safe being outside of my garage door. As soon as workers started leaving and neighbours began driving off, I began to pack away my cleaning equipment as well.

This proves beyond the shadow of a doubt, that as careful as we are, at times we are bound to let our guard down, even for a few seconds. The kidnappers must have been very patient indeed to have waited around for that opening of approximately fifteen seconds.

That's all it took. One was armed with a blade and the other a gun; they entered my garage; my home, my privacy, my safe haven and my life forevermore.

In that moment of sheer terror, all the blood in my body seemed to drop to my feet and I felt my entire body go ice cold. To an unprepared person, when this kind of terror hits, it can stun you into immobility. I was certainly not prepared to deal with a scenario where my life was being threatened. Immediately I thought of my husband and children. I knew that they would be home soon, but thankfully they were safe because they were not present at that point in time. It was my motherly instincts kicking in, as will yours if you are a parent; the instinct to protect your offspring, your loved ones.

My husband and I had often discussed the possibility of a kidnapping occurring in our family and I remember the jokes we made about it. I always said that if I was taken away that he was not to pay any ransom because I would fight to the death anyway. He always agreed, saying he would tell the kidnappers to keep me because he had been trying for years to get rid of me. He joked that this would surely compel them to release me or just to give up the entire plan. We laughed then. It was no joke now, and I no longer wished to fight to the death. The only thought racing through my mind was how I could best survive, otherwise who would take care of my two young children if I was killed?

Despite my terror I was able to assess my predicament. The reality was:
- As a petite female, at a height of only 5 feet, I did not possess any great amount of physical strength.

- There were no neighbours or workers around to hear me if I screamed for help.

- The phone was out of my reach to make any emergency calls.

- The gun was aimed directly at my head so any false move would have inevitably resulted in my death.

- My assailants were dark skinned, over 6 feet tall, muscular and lethally armed.

- I was not trained in self-defence.

Immediately I knew that my chances of surviving a physical fight were slim to none. In my assessment, the odds were stacked up against me, my children and husband were not in immediate danger and so I should cooperate with them and hope that this was a simple robbery and nothing more.

The only thing I could say was the name of **"Jesus"**. It was the only word that came from my lips over and over again. I merely pointed to where my wallet and jewelry were located and begged them not to hurt me. Their response was to indicate I should hush and nobody would get hurt.

They tied my hands and feet with an electrical cord from a set of headphones. My mouth was gagged with one of my husband's ties and my eyes blindfolded with another. I lay on my stomach on the floor of my son's room for what seemed like an eternity. The criminals proceeded to turn my house upside down, rifling through every single closet and drawer that might potentially contain valuables. At this point in time, I could not have cared less if they had taken the entire house and packed it into the waiting vehicle, as long as my family and I were all safe.

My hopes were dashed when a pillowcase was thrown over my head and my feet untied. I knew that they were about to abduct me. I begged, pleading with them through the gag in my mouth; I begged for them to allow me to withdraw all the cash from the various bank accounts. I promised that I would not "squeal" or try to escape – just to please let me go safely. They paid no heed, for their plan was already in motion. I was made to walk down the stairs and into the garage, the door to which remained open. I was verbally threatened, the gun was still jammed against my head and soon a vehicle backed into the garage. I was thrown onto the floor of the vehicle and one of my assailants sat next to me to ensure that I did not try to escape. I knew I did not stand a chance after that, except maybe for the car door.

I was covered with a curtain torn from a window in my own home. Despite having my hands tied I attempted to open the car door. I received some expletives and shoves for trying to escape. My hands were held occasionally from then onwards.

When I realized that the child safety locks were on or the door itself was locked, I suspected that these men were professionals and knew exactly what they were doing and how to be most efficient at their tasks. I closed my eyes; I tried to sleep, only to reawaken and realize anew that this terrible experience was real, my worst nightmare coming true.

It took me a few minutes to fully comprehend the seriousness of my situation. For some reason, I kept expecting to hear sirens behind us and my husband shouting at these evil men to "unhand me." I imagined there would be a sudden crash and he (my husband) would rescue me from the fleeing car. I would then be instantly reunited with my two babies whom I would embrace and never let go. My fantasy faded quickly as the escaping vehicle sped around sharp corners and over speed bumps at a frightful pace. I kept rolling onto the floor and then my captor would yank me back unto the seat again. My head received quite a few hard bangs, as did my chest. The men never spoke; it was almost as though there was a secret understanding of their plan and its quick progression.

There were no sirens, and the nightmare continued. I felt lost and alone, separated from the world filled with people going about their lives as though all was well.

I could not understand how I could be present at one moment and then just disappear without a trace all of a sudden and nobody cared or noticed, with the exception of my family of course. For them the nightmare had just begun, as it would continue for me. I noticed streetlights flying by. I knew I was travelling along the highway. Surely, someone would have noticed this car speeding along; travelling at an inhumane speed. But, of course crazy driving on our nation's highways is a common, daily occurrence so my abduction went unnoticed. At one point, I heard a siren, perhaps an ambulance, a police vehicle or a fire truck; but again, I remained unnoticed.

When their driving slowed, it was further confirmed to me that those men were professionals, as they did not wish to stand out by driving erratically. They simply blended in. The music in the car, however, was turned all the way up; to drown any potential screams presumably. I knew my next opportunity for escape would come while they were moving me from the vehicle to 'wherever'. As terrified as I was, I prepared myself to make a dash for freedom; whatever the cost.

Unfortunately, I remained locked inside of the vehicle with one of my abductors while the driver left us for quite a while. I could hear the voices of women and children and dogs barking, yet I remained lost to the world. I heard the man in the backseat with me knocking on the window glass and pulling at the door handle. He was obviously locked in like me. This confirmed to me the child safety locks were on and these men were clearly professionals who knew about taking such precautions to ensure that I could not escape.

Eventually I was wrapped tightly in the curtain and then dragged out of the vehicle. I was lifted and thrown into a deep hole in the ground. I landed hard and I thoroughly bruised my back, side and head. Now my entire body was aching with a throbbing pain. I was dizzy from the fall and scraped all over. I wondered how I could be treated so vilely, so much like a bag of garbage.

I remained tied, gagged and soaked by falling rain for the rest of the day and into the night. I cried uncontrollably, pleading to know why they had chosen me because we were not wealthy. My captor then recited to me about how many times he had passed by me on my own street, my husband's occupation, the cars we owned and too much information on my children. I momentarily ceased crying, in shock at the knowledge this strange man had about my family. They had targeted us.

They had to have been watching us closely for a while to know so very much about our life. I continued to beg him to free me for the sake of my children. I even asked him if he had children of his own, to which he responded that he had three children. It did not seem to bother him that he was depriving my children of their mother and causing such suffering in their little hearts.

One must always be keenly aware that although criminals are also people, they are not wired the way we are, with moral and spiritual values and a conscience. While they would not want that kind of torture inflicted upon their own families, they can easily inflict it upon others and suffer no remorse. How or why, I still cannot answer.

My tears refused to stop flowing. I was offered pizza and juice. I could not eat or drink; I would have puked. I made an error in judgment there because I was badly dehydrated already and I did not know if I would be offered sustenance again. I did not yet understand the consequences of dehydration combined with intense adrenaline rushes and shivering in the cold.

My allergies were triggered and breathing was extremely difficult because of the gag and blindfold. The stress that my body endured during the first few days of captivity was unimaginable and even today I marvel at the fact that I survived with my sanity intact.

I prayed that the insects that bit into my skin were not poisonous. I was crudely sprayed with insect repellent late into the evening when the bugs came out to play – with me. I smelt the strong stench of garbage and I estimated that I was in some sort of dumping area of a village or community. My skin itched all over with insect bites, but could scratch none of them.

A simple itch becomes sheer torture when you have lost the freedom to relieve it. That torture was quickly becoming unbearable, but the worst torture still was being kept away from my husband and children. I further tormented myself with thoughts of what my family must have been enduring mentally.

I tried to imagine the looks on the faces of my children and parents and worried for my ailing father. I was unsure that he could withstand the news of my abduction. We were never really close but the depth of my love for him I truly felt at that point in time. I would have given anything to be safe in his arms and in my childhood home. I would have given anything to lay my head on my mother's lap and have her tell me that it was all going to be okay in the end.

Again, my fantasies were interrupted by a change in shift of my captors. Another strange man guarded me but he was much rougher on me than the previous one. For just a twitch, he would grab me by the shoulders and shake me roughly.

Unfortunately, I made the error of sneezing and shivering, for which I was slapped and choked and with the use of terrible expletives, commanded to "shut the ***up!" I dared not sneeze again and I dared not rub my nose to prevent myself from sneezing either. I just thanked God Almighty that I did not sneeze anymore – at least for the time being.

My rear end ached terribly from pressing against a tree root or rock. I dared not change positions, so I allowed myself to go numb in that area. When I was finally instructed to stand, I could not. I toppled over in pain and numbness.

Gradually, the circulation and feeling returned as I was hauled off the ground with whispered curses. I was forced to urinate in front of my captor, right on the muddied ground where I sat. I could feel his eyes boring holes into me and it was almost a blessing to not be able to see his face, for I was certain that it would have haunted me for the rest of my life.

I was thoroughly humiliated; me, a shy conservative girl from the street next door to my husband was urinating in the open view of strange men. At this point I was broken; I was shattered. Little did I know that there were even worse things to follow.

Late into the night, I was literally dragged up out of the hole by my arms. Once again, my back took the brunt of the blows, bruises and scrapes. I was told that I would be taken to an 'apartment' where I would spend the night and that I should not worry because 'right now I had to be taken care of'. I used this to my advantage. I understood then that I would be held for at least a couple of days while the ransom was negotiated, so I could not afford to sustain any further cuts or injuries. I lied; I told my captor that I suspected that I had diabetes but I was awaiting my blood test results from the doctor. I thought that they would take better care of me if I had such an illness and this would increase my chances of survival. It was just a thought. I was forced to walk uphill for approximately half an hour.

Being bare feet, I endured a great deal of pain walking through bushes, over asphalt, boulders, gravel and moss, all blindfolded. I sustained several cuts to my feet and I slipped and fell many, many times on the water soaked ground. I was repeatedly yanked upright and shoved forward. Finally, in sheer exhaustion, I fell to the ground, unable to move from pain.

Their solution was simple. I was lifted and thrown across one man's shoulder as though I was weightless while he climbed uphill almost effortlessly.

I remember seeing the faint glow of Christmas lights around people's houses. Other than that, there was only utter darkness.

My captor arrived at a concrete platform of some sort and I was deposited there. I was told to sit still and the two men proceeded to unlock some doors. I was then grabbed and flung inside of a room. I was extremely fearful of being raped, this being my worst-case scenario. Briefly I felt a bit comforted by the warmth of the room I sat in. I shivered in cold and fright and curled into a ball to try to stay warm.

The room was locked and I was left there for a while; I never ceased crying. I grieved to have my husband's arms around me to feel safe, dry, warm and loved. It was not to be. I kept envisioning my children asking for me and crying because I did not show up to see their dances and musical pieces; I kept feeling their soft cheeks rubbing on mine.

Just as I started to warm up, one of my captors returned, entered the room and locked the door. He threw an old worn out towel on me and said that I would have to take a bath and there was no hot water. I begged him not to make me bathe because I felt fine. I lied frantically because I feared stripping in front of this maniac. He insisted, saying his 'Boss' said so; they did not want my cuts and bruises to get infected. I insisted I did not care and instead told him that I would wash all the exposed areas, my arms, legs and neck to prevent infections. For this I was severely treated, slapped, shoved and cursed.

When he proceeded to strip me of my clothing I finally acceded to his wishes. I stripped myself naked, while bursting into a fresh onslaught of tears borne of sheer humiliation and grief. I quickly wrapped myself with the small, worn and torn towel, trying to preserve some semblance of dignity. I was crudely shoved outdoors onto an ice-cold concrete platform and my towel was taken from me. He shoved me to the floor where he had placed a bar of soap and a hard hat to scoop water out of a tub. I crouched low in a failed attempt to hide as much of my body as possible. The wind blew with a vengeance and the water was icy cold; the combination stung my cuts and bruises mercilessly. But what hurt more than that was the knowledge that I was bathing under the open sky with some strange, cruel man staring at my nakedness.

At this point, I realized that the only way I would survive this tragedy was to hold on to memories of my family. Thoughts of them brought a crumb of peace to my mind; enough to ease my incessant crying and trembling. Still my body was weakening terribly and I began to feel very ill. My allergies were a mess, my migraine headache was raging and there was a gnawing nausea that prevented me from ingesting anything.

The blindfold (my husband's tie) was tightened even further and I was handcuffed to a small 'bed'. I was offered a hot cup of tea. This time I was glad for something warm to drink and a few tiny sips helped to warm my body. The momentary pause in my fit of crying resumed as the television was turned on and I heard 'my story' being told on the nightly newscast.

I estimated that I was listening to the 10pm news report as night had fallen hours ago. It hurt to hear my name being spoken as though I was some sort of obscure object lost in a stack of hay. I felt terribly displaced and lost; utterly alone and so desperate to be found by someone – anyone.

As I sobbed, my captor asked me if I would ever stop crying; to which I responded no. I continued to beg him to let me go home to my children. His heart was cold and he calmly said that if he did that, he would be killed. He was immune to the pain I was in and totally oblivious to the agony that my children would have been suffering as a direct result.

The bottom line for him was being paid for grabbing me. I remember the rain poured that night and the memory of the huge drops pounding on the galvanized sheets is still vivid to me. Even now any similar sound causes a terrible reaction in me.

I began shivering again as wisps of cold breeze streamed into the 'apartment'. I curled up into the smallest ball I could to warm up but given the fact that I was chained to the bed; there was only so much room to maneuver.

The television was turned off and my captor left for a while; I however continued to cry. A short time later, he returned and was enraged. He had apparently held a conversation with his 'boss' who informed him that my husband was not being cooperative with them. He paced angrily and cursed my husband for being a stubborn fool. He claimed that he did not really love me otherwise he would not have 'roughed them up'. My husband was rude to them and they obviously thought that they deserved some sort of respect because they held my life in their hands. Because this respect was not shown to them, they lost their temper and their wrath fell upon me.

The wrath I speak of is the unfortunate experience of most, if not all women who are kidnapped. The experience I speak of is rape. Most women shy away from admitting to having endured such a monstrous act, but I choose to speak of my experience. Why? Because, the wider public considers this issue 'taboo', when the truth is that rape is actually so common in any society that it has risen to the level of an epidemic. One must wonder why?

I choose to attempt to inform others of the horrors of living with this memory so that more women will remember to be conscious of their safety and take the necessary precautions. I also choose to speak about rape because, for far too long, women and men have swept this crime under the carpet, hoping against all hope that these problems would simply disappear. It is time that people realize that ignoring a negative situation never solves it, but in fact compounds it. I am attempting to address this issue, among others, affecting women.

Lessons Learned
• There is a hidden emotional toll to be paid during such an experience. It is the sense of being cut off from the rest of the world, abandoned, invisible and unimportant.

• Your memories and your sense of self-worth are the tools you must rely on to get you through those moments of being lost to the world.

• You have value, you are important and you have not been cast off as worthless.

• During an experience such as this the unendurable also becomes survivable; such as being stripped naked in front of strange men; the utter lack of privacy for bodily functions, and the degradation of being physically abused, even being raped.

• These are the stuff of any woman's nightmares. They are all endurable when the priority is staying alive.

• It is a painful lesson to learn but it is a basic truth. Staying alive is the priority.

"I can be changed by what happens to me, but I refuse to be reduced by it."

- Maya Angelou

CHAPTER 4
The After Effects of Rape

While I can now recount my experience of being raped with a certain amount of equanimity, I still cannot look anyone in the eye and say how I 'feel' about it. To this day I find it difficult to open myself up to new friendships and social relationships. There are moments when I cannot meet my own eyes in the mirror. I can no longer walk through a crowd of strangers, or even stand in close proximity to a male; regardless of his race. Being raped damages a woman's self-confidence and her sense of self-worth. Rape is the ultimate violation and criminals know that the fastest and most effective way to subdue, break and tarnish a woman is to rape her. By doing so, they not only hurt her physically, emotionally and mentally but they also hurt her husband or boyfriend, and even her family. It is the extended pain that most people fail to recognize, however, it is a stark reality that survivors of violent crime discover.

Late into the first night of my captivity, a bottle of baby oil was tossed at me and I was instructed to undress. I begged; I begged like never before. I was so tempted to fight to the death, and would have been happy to die in a battle to preserve my dignity and womanhood – but the children. The sound of my son's laughter and my daughter's first word rang incessantly in my brain. I could not fight more than I did but I could beg. I backed away as far as possible and continued to beg, but he was relentless.

He insisted and it was only when he began to pull off my clothing that I humbled myself because I knew I would not survive a solid blow from my attacker.

Who would love my children the way I do? Nobody would. I cried, screamed and begged while slowly pulling apart my clothing with trembling hands. He used the baby oil to lubricate himself and me and grasped my hand to hold him. I cringed, my blood crawled and I felt like maggots were eating me alive.

This feeling persists even now at any recollection of the event. I itch uncontrollably, I scratch at my skin until it is red and painful and showers are a grossly inadequate attempt to cleanse myself.

The kidnapper proceeded to rape me. Every scream, kick and protest on my part was quelled with a large strong hand squeezing my throat. I was choked so severely that night that my throat hurt for over a week after. I could not scream, nor could I fight him off, and believe me I tried, but I failed because of my petite frame and his tall muscular body. My blood crawls even now at the memory of him touching me.

My body was torn and I bled profusely. At the end, I curled into a tiny ball on the mattress and remained still while he took a bath. I was then instructed to go outside and wash myself. I was shoved out into the icy breeze again and I washed myself, almost unconsciously. I remember feeling numb and I could no longer cry. I felt as though I was watching him do this terrible thing to somebody else.

I kept asking myself if this is real, if in fact my worst nightmare had just occurred. I was now swimming in an abyss of despair, darkness and hopelessness. I felt like dirt; like I was the most useless and unworthy being alive.

Rape victims often feel this way; they spiral through a storm cloud of powerful painful emotions and physical reactions. I remained curled up in a ball on the mattress until the kidnapper was ready to move me once more. I cried softly and held on to my aching throat. If I could have seen my neck I am certain that it would have been either red or turning blue and black due to

44

the choking. I am equally certain that I would not have recognized the woman in any reflection. There are still moments when I do not recognize myself in the mirror. I look at my reflection to brush my hair or to dress myself, however, I scarcely ever make eye contact with myself anymore; I barely even remember how I really look – me Debbie. The person I see is no longer a person I recognize. That Debbie has died, and a new person has replaced her. Now, I'm a person as different to myself as any stranger standing next to you in the supermarket.

"Our greatest human freedom is that,
despite whatever our physical situation is in life,
we are always free to choose our thoughts!"
- Viktor Frankl

I am still trying to understand this new Debbie, getting to know her, her habits, likes and dislikes; still trying to decide if I truly like her at all. It is the same for my children and husband. My two children are not the same as they were before the incident and my husband is not the man I married. I am still reacquainting myself with him, his habits, likes and dislikes and learning to love him all over again. He has also had to re-acquaint himself with me, his wife, because I am most certainly not the untouched, innocent woman he married. Even my children have developed new habits and personalities and they often comment on how much I have changed. They are learning to love their new mummy again. Yet the question remains, "*Can I love the new me?*" "*Can my husband love and accept the new me?*" It is a battle that rages every single day and an adjustment we attempt daily, like newlyweds.

"Life is about moving on, accepting changes and
looking forward to what makes you stronger
and more complete."
- Unknown

These changes took place without our permission and yet we are forced to deal with and accept the terrifying results. Both partners in the relationship have to make a conscious choice to either stick it out and give their best shot or take the easier way out and start your life all over again. Even if you stay in the relationship, it is sometimes necessary to pack up what remains of your life and physically move away, to start fresh, away from the reminders of what happened. However, one can never run from one's memories and one can never run from one's self; somehow they always pop up when you least expect.

Thus, I have found that the simpler, less strenuous path has been to simply learn to deal with myself, my marriage and my children upfront instead of having to do constant damage control. I have consciously chosen to confront all the issues, one at a time, accept them and deal with them.

My main priority has been learning to live with myself because I came to the understanding that I would not be capable of handling my husband or children unless I first accepted and put behind me all that has happened to me, and to somehow extract some positives from the ordeal.

"Strength does not come from physical capacity.
It comes from an indomitable will."
- Bruce Lee

Bitter tears are shed every day by women, and men as well, who are raped. Unfortunately, many instances of this crime go unreported because of the stigma attached to it. Clearly it is time that the seriousness of this issue be dealt with at its root cause. As adults in this society, as women, wives and mothers in this society, we can no longer be silent.

We MUST take responsibility and ask ourselves, why are the young men, boys and adult males exhibiting deviant behaviour by committing rapes and extreme violence against women today? Where did we go wrong in raising our boys into men? Fathers, where did you go wrong in raising your boys? While I realize that we can only each do our best, given our individual circumstances, we must step up, all of us, and take charge of the 'unrest' occurring within the male population in our society.

We place great emphasis on education and achieving outstanding academic goals, yet in many instances, we fail to teach our youth vitally important life skills. We fail to equip them adequately with the essential attitudes, values, morals, principles and ethics needed to coexist peacefully with others in this world. We have failed them. We must take the time to teach our young men to be courteous, respectful and gentle with women.

We must teach them conflict resolution skills, decision making skills and anger management skills. How else is this problem to be curbed?

How many more women must suffer this vile consequence? A woman never 'deserves' to be raped; not because of her mode of dress, the time of day or night when she may be out, nor because of any other of her choices. A woman's (and man's) response of 'NO' must be taken at face value and that choice respected. The foundation of a developed nation is developed people.

"It isn't the past which holds us back, it's the future; and how we undermine it, today."
- Viktor Frankl

The burning question in my mind and that of my husband is how do we move on? How does one put behind them such a tragic occurrence and all its repercussions? How can one possibly move forward when there is no justice served? When there is no justice in sight, is closure possible? And for us there was no justice because the kidnappers have never been caught and punished.

Lessons Learned
• By raping a woman, aggressors are not only hurting her physically, emotionally and mentally but they also hurt her husband/boyfriend, and her family at large. This reality is often not recognized by outsiders.

• Side effects of this experience can include PTSD, depression, severe anxiety, self- esteem issues, suicide, guilt, an inability to forgive, anger management, not to mention dealing with the pain of close family members, this especially includes children. There are coping mechanisms such as mediation that can be learned which will help survivors learn to get on with their lives. Even if it helps just one survivor to get a restful night's sleep there is value in that. I credit the success of these mechanisms to Almighty God who gave me insight into myself and healing so I have been able to do so, and to help others suffering similarly.

"But there was no need to be ashamed of tears, for tears bore witness that a man had the greatest of courage, the courage to suffer."

- Viktor Frankl

CHAPTER 5
Surviving

In the midst of any abduction, the dynamics at work are inevitably overwhelming and ever evolving. Great emphasis must be placed on the need to continuously assess the situation; you must be able to adapt to the various situations you may find yourself in. In my particular situation I quickly realized that excessive force would be used to subdue me and to act as a deterrent to any attempt on my part to escape.

When I realized that I was about to be moved again, the numbness I felt overwhelmed me and I honestly did not care if I lived or died. As far as I was concerned, I was happy to die and thoughts of my children, husband and family were far from my mind. I knew it would devastate them to find out that I had been violated, so I vowed that if I did survive this ordeal that I would not tell a soul about that part of my captivity. I made this decision for the benefit of my loved ones. As I contemplated my husband's reaction to news of the rape, I knew that he would most assuredly be crushed and would probably faint in utter devastation. It turned out that I was correct. I had no inkling I would also have to deal with the public reaction to my kidnapping ordeal.

I was told to be quiet and was left alone, shivering on the mattress while arrangements were being made for my move. Still numb from the rape and trauma of my abduction, I moved in a trance-like state from the apartment' into a car. A black cotton mask was placed loosely over my head and the handcuffs tightened.

Although I could scarcely breathe through the thick material, I dared not ask the men to lift it over my nostrils; in fact, I did not care if I suffocated and died; I wished it. I was made to lie on the floor of the car as they raced to my new destination. I vaguely remember thinking to myself that the worst was over and my husband would come through for me and I would be rescued or released. I was sorely mistaken.

I had no idea that my new 'Keeper' would be somebody entirely different. When we arrived I was roughly yanked out of the vehicle and held in a chokehold. My already sore throat and neck were now pounding with a stabbing pain. I was sure that my neck would be broken at any moment.

Words were spoken and I changed hands, given to a rather largely built man. I remember that his hands were unusually huge, hard and rough. He took me inside, still in a chokehold and as he dragged me in, I was sternly warned not to make a sound or I would die. The grip of his forearm around my neck cut off my circulation almost entirely and I felt odd and faint. There was the lone sound of a dog barking and as we drew closer to the animal, I was thrown unto a concrete floor where my head audibly crunched against a wall. I started sobbing once again and I was slapped and told to "shut the***up." I curled up into a ball again because I could feel that the dog was very close to my location. The vehicle left quickly and some sort of dog chain was used to string me up with the handcuffs.

So, now my hands were suspended above my head as I sat on the cold concrete. My new captor effortlessly quieted the dog and then turned his attention to me.

He adjusted the mask above my nose so that I could breathe easier, and for this I was indeed grateful. The next step was to use duct tape to bind the mask tightly around my head and so ensure that I could see nothing. It worked. I did not see even a sliver of light for the next thirteen days.

In fact, he wound the duct tape so tightly that it began cutting off my circulation and I made the unfortunate mistake of telling the 'Keeper' to please not wrap it so tightly because I was feeling dizzy. I was then treated to an outpouring of expletives and a solid cuff to the face. He continued with the task at hand and somewhere along the line I became unconscious. I am still unsure as to how long I was out, but when I awoke, my head and neck were in tremendous pain and the 'Keeper' was desperately slapping me and calling my name.

He was obviously afraid that I had died and he proceeded to loosen the duct tape from around my head, asking me this time if it was comfortable. I nodded slightly and he checked my pulse, after which I was left for a few minutes. When he returned, he asked me if I was raped or hurt by any of the men who grabbed me, to which I reluctantly responded yes.

He assured me that he would deal with them and that I would not be hurt anymore because he had to keep me safe and healthy to be exchanged for the ransom money. He was upset that I was hurt and called someone on his mobile phone; I could not hear his conversation because he moved away. I began to cry again and this time it would not stop until the third day. What followed was the horror of horror stories.

I was dragged into a tiny, unventilated room and chained to the wooden bedpost of a small 'bed'. At that point I was shivering from the cold morning air, despite being in the enclosed room. I lay quietly, still crying but too numb to really feel anything – or so I thought. The 'Keeper' tightly secured my feet with a tie strap and continuously questioned me as to whether I was tampering with the mask over my head or not. As often as I denied this (I was being truthful), he insisted that I was lying and threw a fresh rain of expletives at me whilst shoving me around roughly on the 'bed'. This only served to spur on my fit of crying which intensely annoyed him. He sternly instructed me to shut up or he would have to shut me up. Sadly, I did not anticipate the full consequences of his threat.

Had I been knowledgeable about how to tense my muscles when being bound, I could have saved myself a great deal of agony, but I was not. I could have possibly prevented the painful numbness my feet experienced from the lack of circulation and I would probably have rested a bit more comfortably. I was left to myself for a few minutes but the 'Keeper' returned shortly with a huge, almost hairless dog that he made sniff me from head to toes. He then proceeded to inform me that, in his absence, this animal would ensure that I did not try to escape.

I was warned that if I even thought of tampering with my mask or chains, let alone attempting to run away, the dog would literally eat me alive. I had no reason to doubt him, although I thought at the time that he was only trying to instill fear in me to prevent an escape. Once again, I was proven wrong.

As early morning moved towards full day, I shivered almost uncontrollably from the frosty air (this was in December when the air was cold, even in the tropics). I made the dreadful mistake of asking my captor for something to cover with. I was complacent in thinking that he would be a bit more considerate of my condition given that he pledged to take care of me – at least until the ransom was paid. How misguided I was in this thinking. One can NEVER confidently rely on any humane or compassionate behaviour from a kidnapper.

I am certain that I was visibly trembling with cold so my 'Keeper' could not have said that I was lying. He must have known that I was telling the truth and I am positive that I spoke in a humble voice. However, his response was less than accommodating as he flew into a rage and unleashed a fresh stream of curses. The consequences of that innocent request will remain with me for the rest of my days. His words were, "So you***feeling cold eh? I will warm you up....I will*** warm you up real nice you***."

I immediately attempted to backtrack as he proceeded to spin me over unto my back (I was curled up in as small a ball as possible on my side). But it was too late. In a split second he yanked off the pants I was given to wear by my previous captor, and the T-shirt was pushed upwards to reveal my chest. I begged; I cried and said that I was not cold anymore. Uncontrollably my crying and begging began to turn to screams, and as often as I screamed for mercy I was brutally choked until I coughed and gasped for breath. I was learning; I was learning fast. I knew that there was no way out of this situation, so instead of fighting (all of my energy was depleted anyway) I bit my bottom lip, sobbed as quietly as I could and bore the excruciating pain the best I could while still instinctively fighting. When he was done, I swear I was reeking of his stench and to this day I can still smell his stink.

To this date, I have not come to terms with the rapes. It has done irreparable damage to me and I am lost as to how to overcome the tragedy. There is no one who can look me in the eyes and say that they know exactly how I feel. There is no one to guide me. In my opinion, rape is the worst of human violations possible. I can offer no advice on this to anyone except that I am learning that it is something that one has to figure out on an individual basis and to survive one must find a source of inner strength in order to overcome this devastation of the soul. I know that one must find one's own self-worth and personal identity and value in order to see one's self as worthy of living again. It is the primary requirement for healing.

I lay semi-nude on the bed, still trembling, not from the cold but from shock and numbness. Then I was instructed to wash; I did. My body was broken and my spirit shattered to pieces and the only sensation I could feel was something warm trickling down my legs. I knew that it was blood. I was screaming inside of my head because of the physical agony and I knew that my body was torn. When I returned to the 'bed', I was re-tied; but I was no longer cold.

A short while later, as I regained some sense of feeling and alertness, I struggled to prepare myself mentally for the challenge of enduring my captivity. Every single time the 'Keeper' walked into the room my heart raced and a heart wrenching fear pervaded my body and mind. The next time he walked in, I dared not twitch, although I began involuntarily shivering again. He stood next to me (I could feel his presence near to me) and asked me if I had interfered with the mask over my head. I simply said no to which his response was that I was lying and that I had pulled it off to see where I was. Sensing the rising anger in his voice, I pleaded with him to believe that I never touched the mask. I did touch it but only to free my nostrils for better breathing; not once did I try to look around. I figured that if I did not see anything at all, then I would stand a better chance of being allowed to live. I was right on this count. Experts have since told me that once you've seen your kidnapper or attacker's face and/or surroundings, it becomes more likely that you will be killed because if you escape you can then identify your assailants.

Once again, I begged him to trust that I had no desire to see him or my surroundings and wanted only to be released, to go home. But there was no reasoning with the man; he threatened to 'deal with me'. Deep down I knew what it meant. The 'Keeper' shoved, kicked and slapped me roughly, spun me over again and yanked off my clothing once more. I cried, screamed and begged for him to stop. His only response was that he was going to teach me a lesson in obedience and even offered to release me if I gave him a sweet***.

After a while, I felt my insides rupture as the assault continued mercilessly. Every scream, sob and cry of pain was greeted with a huge hand choking off whatever life I had left. My efforts were useless against his strength and I lost the battle again. Once he was finished, he left me for a few minutes, in shock after the third rape. When he returned, I was made to wash again and the sheet was changed on the 'bed'. I washed and could barely move with the pain I was enduring; the blood poured out and I was unsure as to how many parts of my body were ripped apar and bleeding – other than my spirit. To date, I can still smell his stink and sweat.

How can the human spirit recover from such a heinous violation of their body and soul? How can any woman ever be whole again after such an event? How can she ever look herself in the mirror and see any beauty? One must recognize that there will be an inevitable battle between what one knows and what one feels. One must continue to persevere, as there is no other viable option.

> *"When a man finds that it is his destiny to suffer...*
> *his unique opportunity lies in the way he bears his*
> *burden. At such a moment, it is not the physical pain*
> *which hurts the most (and this applies to adults as*
> *much as to punished children); it is the mental*
> *agony caused by the injustice,*
> *the unreasonableness of it all."*
> *- Viktor Frankl*

Having successfully broken my spirit, the 'Keeper' seemed to calm down and took a softer approach towards me. I believe that he realized that I was not about to escape, that I was simply too weak to even try. I was made to sit up and eat some crackers and given some water. I sipped and ate a miniscule amount. How could one stomach any food after having endured such trauma, pain and anguish? I was physically exhausted, nauseous and shaking but still I could not sleep. Memories of the birth of my two children agonized me; as did memories of my husband and I on our wedding day. I cried uncontrollably throughout the day and prayed for God to take care of my babies (my children and husband).

I worried incessantly about my parents' health and my brother's state of mind. My brother and I had rebuilt our relationship after many years of turbulence and I felt that I was about to lose him again. I did not want to lose my big brother, nor was I ready to say goodbye to my parents and family. I prayed all day and into the night for my husband and children. Somehow I knew that they would be alright – and in some ways my prayers were answered.

Later that night, the 'Keeper' returned and said that my husband was being difficult and that he really did not love me because he was stalling for too long. Not the words I wanted to hear, but the numbness I felt persisted and dulled the anxiety I would normally have felt. I was given more crackers and water; I refused and he tried to encourage me to eat, otherwise I would get sick. Honestly, I did not care to live; not after having been raped repeatedly. He left me alone for the night; under the watchful eyes of his 'dog' who slept on the floor next to me.

I began to realize there was a very real possibility that I would not be freed but slaughtered. Soon I no longer had sufficient presence of mind to even pray, so I lay still and waited for the gunshot or blade to send me into the great beyond. Time passed with agonizing slowness and I was forced to confront myself. It was then that I realized that the most difficult person to coexist with is yourself. No one can torment you as much as you yourself can. I resumed crying that night and could not fall into a slumber despite my exhaustion.

I listened to all of the sounds in my environment and sometime late that night the 'Keeper' returned, settling to sleep outside of the room I was being held in. The next morning, I quietly asked if there was any word from my husband to which he responded no. I was learning to ask permission if I could speak to him. Once he agreed, I asked my questions. I honestly believe that my humility in asking permission to speak made my captor feel more in control than he really was. He felt that he had humbled me and had won some sort of victory over me. I was just trying to avert any further pain and agony.

Again I was forced to eat a few crackers and I accepted a few sips of water. I was incredibly weak and now I felt feverish and strange. The strange sensations I was experiencing were, in fact, my body slowly going into shock. I know that now but at that time, I felt like I was dying; I wished that I was.

That day, the 'Keeper' stayed with me constantly, practically begging me to eat. My only response was more crying and pleading for him not to force me to eat or I would throw up; I threw up anyway. He was obviously growing concerned about the state of my health as he checked my pulse. I realized that my 'Keeper' knew basic first aid – no doubt in the interest of keeping his hostage – me, alive, at least for the moment. Somewhere along the line I may have dozed off in sheer exhaustion, despite my entire body throbbing in pain.

When I awoke, I threw up again and as I lay back down, I felt myself growing very dizzy and faint. The next thing I knew I was convulsing uncontrollably on the 'bed'; so much so that the entire 'bed' shook violently. Upon hearing some sounds from the room the 'Keeper' rushed in and tried to hold me down on the bed. I have no idea what noises I was making and I was oblivious to his presence at that moment.

Apparently he realized that I had gone into shock and he loosened the straps on my feet and hands. After convulsing for some time, I passed out. When I awoke (I am not sure how long after I passed out), he was splashing me anxiously with water and calling me to wake up. He shook me violently again, and eventually I responded. I believed it was the closest I came to dying during my ordeal. I now understand that I had gone into shock from dehydration, anxiety and adrenaline overload. The episode could easily have cost me my life – sometimes I wish that it had. When I settled down, he sternly ordered me to ingest two *Paracetamol* pills (an over-the-counter pain medication) and drink some juice. He was now gentler with me and encouraged me to sleep and relax. I could not; I felt filthy and vile. Later in the evening, he bathed me and allowed me to brush my teeth. I was given oversized pants and a t-shirt to wear but no undergarments. I did not care.

A bit more comfortable now, I did sleep for a short time but was repeatedly awakened by the sound of my husband's voice calling me to come home. Each time I awoke crying hysterically. This apparently won some sympathy from the 'Keeper'. He asked me what I was dreaming about and when I told him, speaking in a quiet voice. He simply said that my life was in my husband's hands and that he was playing with it.

It was unbelievably humiliating to have a stranger bathe me. When this was done for me after each of my children were delivered via Caesarean Section, I felt humbled and embarrassed, but not humiliated. This tore me apart further, having a strange man's hands washing my entire body and continuously seeing me naked. I grew up in a very sheltered and conservative religious environment. This treatment was clearly a violation of my principles, morals and values. He was not gentle, but at the same time he was not unduly rough. The thought of these events still leaves me aghast at the fact that I – Debbie endured such experiences and lived to tell about it.

After surviving my terrible episodes of 'shock', I now had to contend with the mental torture of being held in captivity for eleven or twelve days. Believe me when I say that the mental torture of those days was far worse than the physical torture.

Lessons Learned

• Every time the kidnap victim changes hands they are entering unknown territory and their danger is increased.

• Tensing one's muscles while being bound is a simple trick that results in the restraints becoming slightly looser when the muscles are relaxed. I learned about this technique after I was rescued.

• As I write, this I feel defeated in life; I feel conquered and demolished by the events of my kidnapping. Believe it or not, I still feel guilty about being raped, although I know that it was not my fault. I sometimes, incorrectly, think that I could have somehow prevented the rapes and, indeed, that I could have somehow prevented the kidnapping itself. On bad days the emotional battle still rages on, and I am certain that I will have to fight this battle for the rest of my life. Am I prepared to do so or not? I am not sure that I have what it takes to continue this struggle; yet I must. And so, you must also (for those in similar situations).

*"Life's battles don't always go to
the stronger or faster man.
But sooner or later the man who wins,
is the man who thinks he can."*

- Bruce Lee

CHAPTER 6
Enduring

I was terribly weak and the physical pains I endured made it almost impossible for me to stand. Thus I was forced to use a basin as a toilet. Utter shame ate me alive. As a married woman, I would never use the bathroom with my husband around. I had to have my privacy, but there I was, urinating and excreting before an absolute stranger.

My captor spoke very little, and when he did, he was brief and to the point; most of the time it was to urge me to eat or drink. A dead hostage leaves the kidnapper nothing to bargain with except a bluff and therefore the 'Keeper' was less likely to be paid his share of the ransom money, and so he did his very best to keep me alive, if only barely so.

The crying began again and came in spurts and for prolonged periods. Most frequently, I cried uncontrollably while listening to the blaring radio. Specific songs brought back memories of my family and husband. I listened almost daily to news updates on the radio of my kidnapping case; weeping as the radio hosts all pleaded with the kidnappers to release me for Christmas, if only for my children's sakes.

I listened as though I was outside of myself, as though they were speaking about someone else. I became keenly aware of how fleeting life can be; how little and insignificant one lone human being can be in the eyes of the world. Life continued for everyone else out there. The world did not stop revolving because I was abducted. In fact, after being held captive for a week most people would have forgotten about my 'case'. I had become a mere statistic and I had never felt so totally alone in my entire life. I longed for someone to speak to; for someone to know that I, Debbie Ali was alive and that I did not just disappear into thin air. I recall hearing the faint voices of neighbours milling around outside. It seemed that the sounds of life came from right on the other side of a wall and yet nobody knew that I was right there; or did they?

To this day, I still wonder what would have happened had I decided to take the chance and scream for help. I weighed my options carefully. I concluded that the risk involved was far too great because with the radio blasting at full volume, it was hardly likely that anyone would have heard me.

Additionally, if I was being held in 'a particular area' (an area known for its criminal activities) or its environs, it was highly possible that if I was discovered or heard by someone outside, they would probably turn me back in as a hostage again.

I remembered reading somewhere that kidnappers sometimes paid neighbours to keep an extra eye out for their hostages should they attempt to escape. Perhaps I would have obtained help if I had screamed, but what if someone heard and told my captor; what would he do then? Rape me again, beat me again, and move me again?

I knew that I would not survive any of those options. There was no way I could have overpowered that giant of a man; not five-foot-tall Debbie Ali. So I remained silent for the remainder of my days of captivity.

I waited, listening to a deafening radio which sat directly behind my head. I waited, feeling filthy and itching all over from ant and mosquito bites; I waited, emotionally numb and exhausted; I waited for a bullet or a blade to relieve me of my terror. It never came. Even now I firmly believe that death would have been better than enduring the agony of not knowing what would become of my life every single time the phone rang or my captor walked into the room.

Death would have been the preferred choice to agonize over if I would be violated repeatedly or beaten or mauled by my daytime guard – a huge pit bull dog.

My fears about the dog were realized a few nights later. Although I am a true animal lover, this beast terrified me every time he walked into the room and sniffed me. Many times the animal would jump unto the bed and trample me.

He made unceasing attempts to chew on my ears, toes and whatever body parts he could get at. At some point I began to suspect that the pit bull was only trying to play with me, as if I was a toy to him. However, in his play he could easily have killed me.

For three consecutive nights, that fierce animal was left untied by my captor and mauled me on the bed. I was forced to stay awake and alert so that I could protect my head and chest, my throat, ears, and toes. I waited to feel his long teeth sinking into some part of me; it never came. It was almost as though he was trained not to kill me but to guard and keep me confined. Just once I made the sorry mistake of dozing off into a light sleep. I awakened to the excruciating pain of the dog ripping tufts of my hair out of my head and chewing a hole into the mask I was made to wear. Before I was fully awake, he jumped over me and made a go for my throat. In protecting my throat, I felt the sharpness of his teeth on my hands and, unfortunately, I also felt the size of his head. It was huge. I never knew that a dog's head could be so overpoweringly large. I still have nightmares of a massive head mauling me, and the sight of any pit bull dog makes me shudder inside. Nevertheless, I still love all animals, but surely one can understand my distaste for that particular breed of dog.

As a direct result of a severe lack of sleep for a period of over three or four days, I was even more weakened, though at the time I did not think that was possible. Never in my entire life had I felt so vulnerable, so totally helpless and so completely unable to move, not even to cough.

Finally, I worked up the courage to request a brief conversation with my abductor during which I very humbly asked that he tie the pit bull outside of the room as he was trampling on me and was leaving numerous scratches and cuts along any exposed skin. He agreed and the dog never bothered me again, save the times he entered the room to steal my crackers from my hand or tumble down my water bottle. When he did these things, I was left without 'food' or water for the day or night depending on when he attacked.

Lesson Learned
• Sometimes kidnappers will use animals as extra guards or as a way to torment their captives. It is not the fault of the animal when it is used in this way, although this does not make it any easier to endure, and afterwards it may result in a lifelong aversion to all such animals or a specific breed.

*"Challenge and adversity are meant
to help you know who you are.
Storms hit your weakness,
but unlock your true strength."*

- Roy T. Bennett

CHAPTER 7
When Will It Be Over

Every single time the 'Keeper's' phone rang, my heart pounded and the same questions raced through my mind. Did my husband pay the ransom? Am I going to be released? Did someone call my 'Keeper' with instructions to kill me because my husband did not pay the ransom? How, oh how would they kill me? Would they rape me again and again before killing me? Oh God NO!!

I remember the ringtone of his phone vividly; it was the same one that rang in the Jurassic Park movie; the phone call that saved the lives of the humans. But I waited an eternity for someone to save my life. The human survival instinct is the most primitive instinct there is. It kicks in without you being consciously aware of it; it even enables the human body to withstand the impossible in an attempt to stay alive. The conscious loss of the will to survive surely ends in death; I was to learn that not very long after.

At this point in time, however, only thoughts of my two children entered my mind and the vision of their little innocent faces crying for 'Mummy' gave me the courage to survive the nightmare I was in. Frequently I found myself disassociating from the world around me, it felt as if I was dreaming, watching all of these events unfold in someone else's life. This could never be happening to Debbie Ali!

There was no way that God would allow these horrible things to happen to me. I grew up in Church and my Lord had always been a critical part of my upbringing and beliefs. I loved the Lord with all of my heart and soul; I always tried to do the right thing. I never cheated, lied, stole, drank, smoked or gossiped - so how could this be happening to me? Even now, years later, the horrors of that time seem like a movie, like someone else's life. Perhaps it will always be that way.

Oddly, my two very young children (at that time) seemed to come to terms with what occurred far faster and better than my husband and I ever anticipated.

Perhaps this is because they were, as much as possible, insulated from the worst parts of what was happening, and afterwards from the details of my ordeal. The pain of my husband and family as they negotiated with the kidnappers were all kept from them. Or perhaps it was God answering the prayer of a mother to protect her children physically, emotionally and mentally from the full effects of such a traumatic event. Whichever it was, I thank God that they were, and continue to be, as resilient as they are. I thank God Almighty that he has preserved some semblance of their childhood and innocence.

The stink of the dog, the stink of a makeshift toilet, the stink of a lone sweaty man invaded my nostrils day and night and for many, many months after I was eventually released from captivity. The sounds of the dogs barking, the squeaking of the door, the horrid ringtone of his mobile phone, his snoring and even the music at the beginning of the nightly news at 7pm, continued to terrorize my very existence long after I was returned to my family.

Lesson Learned
• Disassociation is a common response to a traumatic event. It allows the brain a respite from the stress of coping with an unimaginable circumstance. It can, however, hinder the recovery process because it interferes with the ability of the mind to properly process events and put the trauma fully in the past.

*"Success, like happiness,
is the unexpected side effect of
one's personal dedication to a cause
greater than oneself."*

- Viktor Frankl

CHAPTER 8
Sharing Our Worlds

Time was elusive to me during those days so I'm not sure when this particular incident occurred, but it was late one evening when the 'Keeper' returned to check on me.

After I was allowed to use the toilet, I was offered the usual crackers and water. I refused to eat.....my kidnapper did not understand why I was not hungry or thirsty and he grew angry. He tried to force the crackers down my throat, which only resulted in loud outbursts of hysterical crying on my part. I was almost screaming so he gave up and left in frustration. Why was I unable to eat when I should have been famished?

I know it was a Sunday because the music on the radio was of a more soothing nature that evening. Earlier that day I had heard my wedding song on the radio and that was all I could take. My sanity almost went out of the window.

Chunks of memories of times with my beloved husband began to overwhelm me. Our first dance ever, which was at my brother's wedding, our first kiss, our wedding night and all the promises we made to each other; the birth of our children and everything in between. The anguish was unbearable and I began convulsing, deluged by tears and emotional pain. The thought of never seeing his smile, smelling his cologne or lying in his arms was....I can find no words to describe the indescribable. Even his annoying habits of leaving his socks inside of his shoes or all over the house....suddenly none of those habits seemed so horrible.

When the 'Keeper' returned, fortunately in a calmer mood, he tried again to coax me into eating. I suppose a dead hostage is of no use when it comes to negotiating a ransom.

When he realized that I still refused to eat or drink and was inconsolable, my kidnapper hugged me.

He actually put his arms around me and tried very hard to calm and comfort me. I took no comfort in his arms; in fact I was repulsed but so great was my emotional agony that I was oblivious to his physical contact – minus sexual intonations.

Automatically, I apologized for not eating and honestly, I still cannot believe that I told him I was sorry for upsetting him by refusing to eat and drink. In hindsight I realize that my words of apology were all signs of humility on my part and his perceived role of 'master'.

Once I calmed down a bit, I drank a little water and he asked why I was crying so hysterically (though not in those exact words). I began weeping again and told him about the reminder of my husband. Before I knew it, I was describing to him how my husband and I met, fell in love and got married, about the two perfect children we were raising.

It was at this point the real conversations began and I was forced to see the reality of his world, and he was forced to see the terrible reality of what he had done to my world.

We talked for hours on end and like "Daniel in the Lion's Den" my Lord had shut the mouth of the beast so I could no longer be harmed.

This poor soul knew nothing of what a family life was like. He had never experienced the love of parents or friends; for him it was 'kill or be killed' 'steal or starve'. It was a whole other world for me and I was certainly moved by the hardships he endured growing up – hardships that I was spared.

"No man should judge unless he asks himself in absolute honesty whether in a similar situation he might not have done the same."
- Viktor Frankl

Pretty soon the pit bull entered the room and my kidnapper proceeded to scratch him and pet him lovingly. I was oddly surprised that he could show such open affection to his animal. He left for a few hours that night with the radio turned on and the dog safely tied just outside of my room. While I cannot say that I slept comfortably that night, whatever shut eye I did get was a bit more restful.

I awoke at some point during the night when the 'Keeper' returned. The terrible whisper of the screeching door caused my heart to pound uncontrollably and again thoughts raced through my mind as to whether this was 'it'....was I about to take a bullet or a blade?

From that night onwards, every single night, my captor slept on the tiny bed with me... I will never know why but my suspicions tell me that he was beginning to take quite a liking towards me.

It was terribly uncomfortable and I had to press myself into the tiniest of spaces to accommodate his huge frame. I remember that he always slept with his shoes on and his snoring kept me awake most nights – I was thoroughly starved for sleep.

Every night, I would smell his odour and his breath, but never the smell of alcohol or cigarettes. Every night as his body touched mine on the bed I was repulsed. To keep myself from throwing up I would vividly recall the smell of my two children; the smell of the baby powder they used – lavender scent; and the body lotion creamed on them after their bedtime bath. Then they would snuggle against my arm, tummy, chest, and butt.... wherever they could, and little did I know that one day I would be drawing on the memories of those smells, sounds and touches just to keep my sanity.

I recalled the tough guy voice my son would imitate when showing me football moves and how he would bicycle kick the ball into the net and then imagine the crowd going wild with his amazing trick! After this, he would show me his victory pose which was that of Ricardo Kaka, or David Beckham and he'd lift his Manchester United or AC Milan T shirt and underneath would be written 'I love Jesus' on his skin.

I often found myself smiling at his childish move and I dreamed his big dreams along with him – he knew that I believed (and always will believe) in his dreams of becoming a professional footballer and I would be proud of him no matter what he decided to pursue.

My 'big son' as I would fondly refer to him, would have my undying support in all that he did; at that point I was determined to live through this horror so that I could see him play his first professional football match. Nothing was going to stop that from happening.

It was thoughts like these that kept my will to survive alive and kicking, despite my agony, humiliation, hunger, weakened state and uncertainty. I remembered the very first moment I laid my eyes on my most manly handsome son. I remembered reading him his favourite Bible story, "David and Goliath". He still loves to hear it. Over the years I read him tons of stories, and as a writer I concocted my own series of 'Big Son stories' which I narrated off the top of my head. He would always smile, giggle and hug me and as he grew older he would always promise to "take care of his Mummy". He had always promised to protect me from everything 'bad' in this world. My precious son, 'faithful companion' – the meaning of his name.

> *"The successful warrior is the average man,*
> *with laser-like focus."*
> *- Bruce Lee*

Other nights, sharing a tiny bed with this stranger, memories of my baby daughter kept me sane. It kept giving me a reason to live to 'see' another day; to live to fight another day. The softness of her skin and her little giggles that were so full of innocence and joy brought me a bitter sweet comfort.

The mere thought of never touching her tiny feet or painting her toenails during a 'girls' night' was nearly unbearable. But I was determined to bear the unbearable to see her petite face, large mesmerizing eyes and long eyelashes again.

I remembered getting into an argument with my then five-year-old baby girl on how to get her dead straight hair to stay up like the other girls. Lying there in that filthy bed I could still laugh at the memory of her frustration that her hair would not stay put. I recalled her sucking her last two fingers on her left hand while taking comfort in her '*blankie*' as she fell asleep. As she slipped into dreamland, her two tiny fingers would slowly fall out of her pink lips and dribble would take its place. I would always, always smile at her, turn her onto her side and pull her hair away from her face and neck. In doing so I would see and gently soothe the tiny, baby hairs that lay at the back of her neck in her sleep; she would smile in dreamland. I cried that night. I shed bitter tears because I would have given both my limbs to feel those baby hairs on her little neck again – just once more.

Now I cherish every opportunity I have to tickle her, sniff her neck and play with the hair at the back of her neck. The argument however, continues on how to get her straight hair to stay up in a bun...Now, just like I did then, I blame it on her father's genes, his hair is as straight as needles.

"Decisions, not conditions, determine what a man is."
- Viktor Frankl

Other nights, with this man lying next to me, mosquitoes biting me everywhere, feeling filthy, I dreamt of soaking in a steaming hot tub and scrubbing myself until my skin fell off.

Every time his phone rang; usually just after midnight, I would jump; afraid to be hopeful, and terrified of the contents of the conversations. Those late-night calls would always be answered beyond my earshot. Several times he re-entered the room grumbling to himself, annoyed that my husband was being difficult and the police presence at my home was "getting the boys jumpy."

I would try to soothe his fears by feeding him bits and pieces of what I thought might have been useful information to them. I gave tidbits such as what my husband's salary was at the time (which was, of course, not accurate) and how we invested most of our earnings into the renovation of our home and our monthly expenses were quite large with the kids attending a private school. To my horror he also knew which private school they attended. But the Lord kept me calm and patient.

Pretty soon, the 'Keeper' began to realize that we were not as wealthy as they had originally thought, and his heart began to soften towards me. After one late night call, he rushed back into the room, rather excited, and told me that I might be going home that night. Needless to say my heart raced in equal excitement. The 'Keeper' hugged me tightly and told me not to cry anymore that I might see my children that very night. I began praying that nothing would go wrong with the drop off of the ransom money; the details about which I knew nothing and of which the kidnapper would divulge nothing.

Moments later his phone rang again, but when he entered the room, he was impatient. He said that my husband had some of the money; they still wanted more, and he said that he would try to raise some more ransom money but he had to be sure that I was alive. However, there was no way he would allow me to speak to my husband; how I longed to hear his voice.....something familiar and warm. The end result was that my husband would relay a question to the kidnapper who would obtain an answer from me; an answer which only I would know. He asked the names of my best friends from my time at Teaching College. I quickly told him the answers and the message was relayed to my husband. My kidnapper disappeared for the rest of the night. I was too excited to sleep and I waited impatiently until his return during the daylight hours.

He was angry, the delivery was not successful as there were too many police involved and this enraged his cohorts. My 'Keeper' was frank with me and told me that 'they' just wanted to finish me off because this 'job' was taking too long and there were too many officers involved. Terror wreaked havoc in my heart.

I was sure I would never see my babies again. He left me all alone for the entire day without offering me my usual portion of crackers and water. Nor was I allowed to use the toilet. I was in total despair. It was my trust and hope in my Lord and Saviour Jesus Christ that got me through that day.

Lesson Learned
- There are techniques that can be learned which allow a survivor of abuse to use positive memories of sights, smells and sounds to recondition their negative thoughts. This is a skill I have mastered over time and I worked long and hard to draw upon very specific positive and happy memories using all of my senses, and to replace specific negative

memories from my experience. It is a lengthy and time consuming process that requires dedication and patience but is almost guaranteed to work.

"In the middle of a difficulty lies opportunity."

- Albert Einstein

CHAPTER 9
The Conversation Continues

Utterly alone, chained and unable to move about, throughout the day I was inflicted with intense stomach cramps. I was afraid that I would soil myself. In an effort to ease my physical discomfort I experimented with mental exercises. The method I used involved colours and deep concentration, a technique I had learned through reading. It got me through the day, but when I heard the door screech open that evening, I could not have been happier. To me it meant relief. I was in agony that day struggling to keep my bladder and bowels under control. Since then I make it a point to never 'hold it'. I hate the discomfort of that sensation and as long as I have my freedom, I swear, nobody or nothing will prevent me from using the washroom whenever I need to. Sounds ridiculous but trust me...when simple privileges and rights are withheld from you, you learn to cherish them.

That evening I was allowed to bathe again in the icy water and brush my teeth. Sometimes it amuses me that nowadays, every chance I get, I take a shower and brush my teeth, kill a mosquito or scratch an itch. None of that was funny at the time though.

Once I was a bit more comfortable, I was given clean clothes that were five times my size but no undergarments. I was really worried by now because I knew that my kidnappers were becoming more impatient, and knowing my husband as I did, I was faced with the stark reality that he would give them as difficult a time as possible to 'close the deal'. That night my kidnapper and I talked again and oddly enough the topics he was most interested in were religion and my relationship with my husband.

While I did see this open line of communication as being a strategy to win his approval, and possibly influence him to 'free me', I was also being myself. I was just being the person that God made me to be, friendly, warm, empathetic and loving (and I say this in all humility).

That night, I obeyed God's calling, unknowingly of course, as I told him all about the love of Jesus Christ. He knew of Jesus but had no personal experience with the love of Christ. He asked me why I believed in Jesus and how I was so sure that he is as real as I described. I explained the best I could have and answered all of his questions. My captor asked me if I hated him; my very honest response was a resounding no. He was extremely surprised at my reply and he asked me why not; because of course I had every reason on earth to hate him for raping me repeatedly and causing me so much physical agony and torture. But, that was just it; I had every reason on earth.... not heaven. Not in God's Kingdom. In God's Kingdom, grace, peace and forgiveness are ever present.

My reply was that, while I did not think that the things he had done were correct or moral, I did not hate him and I could not hate him. It was the truth... I could not hate him then and I cannot hate him even now. Such is the power of the love of Jesus Christ... the power to love the unlovable and to forgive the unforgivable.

As his voice began to quiver with emotion, he held my free hand tightly and almost shouted "why" at me because he simply could not fathom my acceptance of him after his horrid behaviour. Again, without giving it a second thought, I told my kidnapper that Jesus did not come into the world to be its judge but to be its Saviour. Thus, if Almighty God Himself refused to be a judge to the sinners; then who was I, a sinner myself, to cast judgment on others. After all, "None is without sin..."

"The more one forgets himself - by giving himself to a cause to serve or another person to love - the more human he is."
- Viktor Frankl

This simple, sincere explanation baffled the 'Keeper' and I do believe that I heard sobbing in his voice. He then proceeded to apologize profusely for the rapes and for torturing me so badly. I told him that all was forgiven and he should not worry about it; I also told him that he needed to forgive himself and to ask God for His forgiveness. He doubted that he would be forgiven by God because he claimed to have led an entire lifetime of crime and hurting innocent people like me. Looking back I tend to question what I really meant by forgiving my torturer. Perhaps it was my way of letting go of any hate I would have harboured against him and so spare myself all of that negativity.

Perhaps 'forgiveness' was just a word I grew up learning. Then again, maybe I somehow understood that my captor had no real experience with the love of God and so made poor choices, and maybe I felt like I needed to excuse him for his ignorance. That does not mean I do not want to see justice served for their crimes against me. I do.

At this point, the 'Keeper' noticed the scapular that I wore on a string around my neck. After stealing all of my valuables, including my platinum wedding ring, here was this 'criminal' asking my permission to keep this symbol of my faith. I asked him why he wanted it, because financially it was worth nothing. He said that it would be very valuable to him because every time he looked at it he would remember me – his friend. I was astounded; his friend?

How could he consider me his friend? I removed my scapular and placed it in his hand; he held my hand for a minute or two and told me that he would think of me whenever he looked at it. I told him to use it as a reminder that it is never too late to ask God for forgiveness for his past, and that God would wipe his slate clean so he could start his life all over again and abandon a life of crime.

The 'Keeper' then confessed that all he grew up learning about was how to take advantage of those who 'had' so that he too could 'have'. But it was his last words that brought him to tears; he said that he had never met a woman like me before; and if he had some twenty or thirty years before, he would never have been involved in a life of crime. He opened my handcuffs and told me that I was free to go. When I asked why, he said that I was now his friend and he was not going to allow anybody to hurt me anymore and he would deal with his partners, even if it meant his own death. He said that a friend does not chain a friend and do things to make them unhappy. This said, he unbound me totally and left the room.

I sat in stunned amazement at what had just transpired. Could it be that this hardened criminal was, in fact, a human being as well, and not the total monster I initially made him out to be? Could it be that he was who he was because of how he was raised and the type of environment he was raised in? Could it be that this was God's way of bringing salvation to a lost soul; through me? Questions swirled through my mind as I struggled to comprehend this new reality. I was totally free to go. He had even tied the dog way outside, away from my reach. Why was I still sitting on the bed?

"Just as a small fire is extinguished by the storm whereas a large fire is enhanced by it - likewise a weak faith is weakened by predicament and catastrophes whereas a strong faith is strengthened by them."
- Viktor Frankl

I rationalized my inability to move. I knew that wherever I was being kept, there were other people around, neighbours if you will. I also knew that if my suspicions were correct and I was in the slums, then I would surely be seen and/or caught and brought back to the room.

After all, I could not even be sure that this was not just a trick to see what I would do. But then why would he put himself in such a risky position? It all made no sense to me.

Ultimately, I decided that, being as weak, delirious and lost as I was, there was no guarantee that I would make it out alive and there was also no guarantee that I would not be caught by other criminal elements and taken advantage again. I somehow felt a sense of comfort being in that room at that point in time; even if it meant death. At least there was someone and something familiar to me, rather than some unknown ambush awaiting me outside, against which I did not physically stand a chance.

Then my mind careened in another direction. If I did in fact escape successfully, then what would happen to the 'Keeper'? He would most certainly be killed for allowing me to escape. This meant that his death, his blood, would be on my hands and my conscience forever. I was not willing to live with those regrets and consequences.

I also thought of God's word that he did not come into this world to condemn it but to save it from death. Therefore, who was I to condemn this man to certain death if I did in fact choose to run away? What if God put me in this position to save his soul and then I let him die? I would be held accountable for his death – technically. I remembered that Jesus could have saved himself from being crucified on the cross at any time that He wished, but He allowed himself to be beaten, ridiculed and put to death (though innocent of all misdeeds) so He could save the lives of sinners.

Jesus did this because God the Father commanded it and though He was faced with a difficult challenge as a human being, a path of fear and suffering, He chose to follow the will of God. In the end the victory was and continues to be His. The predominant thoughts going through my mind were the thoughts that God Almighty put there. If Jesus could humble himself enough to be wrongfully crucified and humiliated, then who was I to try to escape a similar fate?

After all, I could be killed at any time by the kidnappers. The Bible did say that "those who wish to follow the example of Jesus Christ and to truly love Him should be prepared to suffer as He did." I was prepared. I loved my Lord beyond anything imaginable, and whatever my fate was to be, I was quite prepared to face it; knowing that I had saved the life and soul of a 'sinner' or at least done my duty as a follower of Christ by telling him, and more importantly, showing him the power of the love of Jesus Christ. I stayed put.

I did not even remove my mask to look around the room. I have no idea why I did not at least do that. Perhaps I thought that if I survived this experience that image would haunt me.

Very late into the night, the 'Keeper' returned, very quietly this time though. I heard a deep sigh, almost of regret, as he sat quietly on the bed next to me. I could tell that he was looking at me and I asked him if he had heard anything from my husband in a soft voice. His response was a soft explosion of expletives directed towards me, all geared towards trying to figure out why I was still sitting there, in captivity, when I was given the opportunity to go home to my family. My response astounded him, as it did me.

As I quoted from the Bible, the hardened criminal beside me was moved to tears. He simply could not fathom that after he had brutally raped, beaten and humiliated me that I would consider his life ahead of my own and the happiness of my family. He did not understand the principle of 'faith' or as I prefer to term it 'knowing' the power of God.

I proceeded to explain to him that although I could have run away and gone home to be with my family, my beloved children, had I done that, I would have been putting the things I cherished the most in this world ahead of what God wanted me to do. Had I done that, God would probably have taken my most prized possessions (my husband and children) away from me anyway. For it is written, "Seek ye first the Kingdom of Heaven and all other things shall be added unto you."

In hindsight I believe that this was the ultimate test of my love and dedication to God Almighty, to see if I was truly suited to do his bidding. I do believe that I passed the test. I grew up always loving God more than anybody and anything else, and like Abraham I was placed in a position where I had to choose to hold on to what I loved most on earth, my children and family, or to do the will of God.

Abraham, though with a broken heart, chose to obey God; as I did. To date I firmly believe that because of this sacrifice, which Jesus gave me the strength to make, I was allowed to meet the Saints in Heaven but I will explain that encounter in a later chapter.

The kidnapper was moved beyond words once more and he asked me again if I would not change my mind and just leave. I refused and his question to me was, "What kind of woman are you to save my life when you should be thinking of saving your own?" I did not give it a thought then, but as I was told once released, "You are a true woman of God." I fervently hope that somewhere along the line I touched this man's heart, allowing God's glory to shine through, and I sincerely hope that wherever he is now that he remembers me and all that I said, and that he still knows that it is never too late for God to wipe his slate clean.

Although I knew that I was obeying God, I still wondered about my own fate. That night the 'Keeper' and I talked some more and he thought that it was so special that my very first boyfriend was the man I ended up marrying. He thought it was amazing that we shared a commitment to each other and held on to our marriage all these years without being unfaithful. He never knew that such a thing as a committed marriage existed and lasted. He said that he hoped he would find someone like me one day to marry.

Oddly, he even added that if he had met me a long time ago we would have been the best of friends. He actually laughed and tried joking with me, but my sorrow was too great to manage even a smile. This was when he asked what kind of music I liked, which, of course, is Rock music.

Since he was not too familiar with rock songs, he was at a loss but tried to hum one rock song he remembered liking from the 80's. I was not sure what song it was but I tried to figure it out for him; of course he continued to encourage me.

It was actually a light moment and I eventually told him the name of the song. He asked me to sing it for him. I backed out right away, because I have never sung for anyone before, including my own husband, and he expected me to sing for him? Now way Hosea! He nudged and poked me, even tried tickling me to sing it until I eventually gave in with much fuss. I sang the first verse of the song and he laughed and jokingly told me he knew why I did not want to sing. I managed a smile and a little chuckle. Who would have thought?

He said that I had the most beautiful smile he had ever seen and that he would make sure that I lived to smile even more when I saw my children again. He vowed to protect me with his life, because I was willing to sacrifice my own to save him. He hugged me and attempted to leave without tying my hands and feet. I actually raised my voice at him to handcuff me and tie my feet because if his 'partners' ever discovered his leniency towards me they would kill him and or me. The 'Keeper' refused, claiming that I was his friend, in fact the best friend he had ever had, bluntly refusing to tie me.

I threatened to scream, and he eventually gave in and very loosely handcuffed me to the bedpost but refused to tie my feet again. I even got an old towel to cover my upper body with that night. Before he left though, he apologized profusely for hurting me and more so for raping me. He said that he would regret it for the rest of his life. He left and I hoped that that would be the night I would be set free. It was not to be.

Lessons Learned
• One of the most important lessons I learnt during those two weeks was letting go of my dire situation and allowing the Almighty to take control of my mind, body and soul.

• This experience also brought home to me the true meaning of forgiveness and how it is so important to completely let go of a negative experience. This includes forgiving oneself, which can sometimes happen much more slowly.

• I also learned about being truly compassionate towards individuals who have endured hardships through no fault of their own. Being able to see a criminal's perspective for the first time taught me a much needed lesson. It is easy to point fingers, but that is just judgmental behaviour. It is also important to note that forgiving someone for horrific behaviour does not automatically mean that justice is not needed or required for healing. All of this bearing in mind that justice is very different to revenge.

91

"And once the storm is over, you won't remember how you made it through, how you managed to survive. You won't even be sure whether the storm is really over. But one thing is certain. When you come out of the storm, you won't be the same person who walked in. That's what this storm's all about."

- Haruki Murakami

CHAPTER 10
Giving Up

That same night, the 'Keeper' returned with no good news, gave me a hug and said to keep the faith before settling to sleep on the bed with me. His words were of no comfort to me and when I finally dozed off I dreamt vividly of the things I was missing. I dreamt of the smell of my husband at night in our bed and how the two kids would jump into our bed and trample all over us, with my little girl settling down on her daddy (her property), and my son snuggling by my side. I dreamt of the four of us crammed into one Queen sized bed and the way my son would carelessly fling his arms and legs all over the place waking up everyone. The way my tiny little daughter could snore loud enough to wake up the entire neighbourhood and the way my husband would 'hook' my feet and drag them across the bed to intertwine with his.... only then would he fall asleep.

I dreamt sweet dreams of my grandparents whom I loved dearly, and cousins who taunted me mercilessly as a child (lovingly of course) because I was always the tiniest person around. The games we all played as toddlers, climbing trees, running races, picking mangoes from trees, picking guavas and then looking for worms in them....after we ate more than half. I dreamt of the days growing up with my brother, without whom I would never have passed mathematics. He was the only person on earth who could muster the patience to teach me high school math.

That night I dreamt sweet dreams of my teenage years, memories of house parties and the boys that liked me. I remembered those days of dancing and joking, cutting class (but consistently getting some of the best grades), playing cards and running rings around a particular teacher whose class we all hated to attend. I even dreamt of the time I was put out of my French class because my teacher Ms. Hem Lee thought that I was wasting my potential (all because I hated French).

Of course, music was a huge part of my life, as it still is today, and my favourite band played the best music in these heavenly dreams....Def Leppard; my all-time favourite band and all-time favourite music. As a teenager I had often dreamt of meeting the band members and attending their concerts. There was always something about British culture that appealed to me....maybe it was the accent, but their music helped to save my sanity during my captivity. With the radio constantly blaring all kinds of noises and talking in my head day and night.... all of which I hated, the only thing I could do to bring some semblance of peace of mind, was to sing Def Leppard songs in my head at night and out loud during the day. Whenever I heard a particularly irritating song or announcer over the radio, I would sing Def Leppard songs to drown them out. This soothed my soul.

With that said, the name of Jesus was constantly on my lips and prayers were continuously on my tongue – if only to see my babies one more time. To keep my will to live, I fed off the memories of my past and planned all the wonderful things I would do once I was released.

I promised myself that if I lived I would be more bold and adventurous in life, I would try different foods and drinks, I would pursue God's work and my writing with renewed fervour and I would make my marriage a perfect one.

I planned to reunite with old friends, spend more time taking care of myself instead of everyone else. I would stick to my exercise routine and dress better. I even planned to try a few forbidden acts. I'll leave that one to the imagination. But as the days dragged by and my body grew weaker, so did my mind. There came a point when even thoughts of my children and husband were unable to sustain my peace of mind and ability to think coherently.

Slowly, I began to fade away. There were voices around me calling me by name; none of whom I recognized. I heard sounds and music that were not present and at times I answered these voices but got no further response from them. I felt like I was literally losing my mind. My body ached, my head ached and I was beginning to feel like I wanted to die. Without consciously knowing it, I had lost the will to live.

I remember at one point I told my brother's wife, my sister-in-law Hema, to take care of the children because they would need her love and attention, and I knew both she and my brother loved them as their own kids. I told my mother, whom I missed terribly, not to worry (as she always does), because all would be well. To my father I said that I loved him and we would meet again, but to my children and husband I said nothing; saying goodbye was far too painful.

I said these things in some kind of a trance-like state; I was conscious, yet not fully aware of my immediate surroundings.

That evening when my 'Keeper' arrived to feed me, he brought a sandwich which I refused to eat, and I refused the water too. Perhaps it was the way I refused that made him concerned and he pleaded with me to eat so I would live. I had stopped talking altogether and as hard as he tried to coax me into singing again or talking about music and Jesus or my children – nothing worked. It was strange; like being there and knowing he was there and understanding everything he was saying but I was somewhere else at the same time, and so was unable to properly respond. I did not fully realize it then, but I was dying; I was dying because I was tired, exhausted from the trauma, rapes, beatings, hunger, dehydration and from doing God's will. I was dying because I no longer wanted to live. I wanted to go home; but where was home?

Lesson Learned
• Def Leppard - It is my heartfelt wish to meet this band that I admire so much. To let them know that they should never take for granted that their music is just music for the sake of making music, money and moving up on the Billboard Charts. I would like them to know that in many, many ways their music became a part of my soul during my kidnapping.

Their music kept me sane for my children. In fact, their music continues to help keep my sanity intact. Whenever I feel overwhelmed or memories come flooding back, I listen to one of their albums and I feel better. Sometimes my kids complain that it's all I ever listen to (though they have come to love it just as much) but that band and their music are precious to me.

*"Defeat is in your mind.
Resilience is in your soul."*

- Keri Murphy

CHAPTER 11
The Edge of Life

That night my 'Keeper' panicked; I could faintly hear it in his voice. He checked my pulse and then called someone in my presence for the first time. I heard him say on the phone that they should settle up that very night because he did not think that I would live much longer. He said two days – tops.

I seemed to be fading in and out of consciousness or was it sleep? Still unsure as to what was happening to me I began to let go of the love I held so dear for my husband, children and family. I started to let go but was jolted back to reality by my kidnapper's hand gently slapping my cheek. He lifted the mask a bit so I could breathe a little better and tried to get me to drink a little. I did. He began fanning me in an attempt to revive me and broke off tiny pieces of a sandwich for me to eat. I ate it unwillingly.

I believe what really worried him was the fact that our conversations had stopped and I was not responding to any kind of stimuli, including changing the radio station to my favourite 95.1FM 'The Rock'. When he realized that even the rock music and familiar voices of the radio hosts did not evoke any reaction, he called someone again and told them to take whatever was offered and end it.

I seemed to have settled into some kind of slumber and my breathing was steady (I know because he checked my pulse beat); then he left. I slept, or so I thought.

When I awoke from what seemed like a very 'deep slumber' I knew that somehow, someway, everything would be okay and that this nightmare would be coming to an end very soon.

Sometime later that night I heard the 'Keeper's' phone ring, but the sound did not strike such fear in me as it usually did.

I became aware that he was feeling very frustrated. My husband had raised some more ransom money and all parties were prepared to finally 'close the deal' but my husband had requested evidence that I was indeed still alive.

I found out later he did not believe that I could have survived that long in captivity. So once more questions were relayed, the answers to which only I knew. The questions were, "*Who is my all-time favourite actor? What is the name of my kids' swimming teacher? What was the code my husband and I used to say 'I love you' without actually saying I love you*?" I almost laughed at the last question.

However, there was a problem that I was unaware of; my 'Keeper' was illiterate. He could neither read nor write and since there were three questions posed, he needed to write the answers and he simply could not. He kept asking me to repeat my answers and to spell the names of the persons requested....a name as simple as TOM CRUISE (who is my all-time favourite actor). I could tell that he was struggling to write 'Tom' because in true childlike fashion, he was saying the letter 'Tttttt' while trying to 'draw it'. After a minute or so of trying to get the one name correct, he gave up, threw the pen/pencil across the room and crumpled the paper. Instead he opted for me to record my answers to the questions using a voice recording device. I did so painlessly. It was after he recorded the information that he laughed at me as he could not believe that my favourite actor was Tom Cruise. Of course, I defended 'my boy', saying that he was a brilliant actor and from all reviews a truly wonderful person at heart, and a great father. My 'Keeper' laughed even harder and thought that Tom Cruise was such a 'pretty boy' and not a rough and tough man like himself. In response to the code between my husband and I for saying "*I love you*" without actually saying the words, I explained to him that we would say "*elephants shoe*". He was baffled and asked what an elephant's shoe has to do with saying I love you. He then tried saying it out loud, and after a few attempts it made sense to him. He laughed heartily at the trick and thought that it was brilliant...although he did not say it in words, his lips would have moved like he was saying "*I love you*". My kidnapper held my hand, squeezed it and said that he would be back with the response and final arrangements for my release. He urged me to keep hope and he left for what seemed like an eternity, while I writhed and stewed in my own sweat.

I had learned from experience that the tiny room in which I was being kept was devoid of any ventilation whatsoever, so during the day I would sweat out any fluid I had taken in, and at night it was icy cold. My challenge was to preserve as much fluid as possible during the day or I knew I would die of dehydration or go into shock again. I did all that I could not to cry because, of course, it would mean a loss of fluids. To prevent myself from crying in despair, I would sing Def Leppard's music in my head all day and all night and dwell on memories of my past as a young single woman when my life was simple and very happy.

To prevent myself from sweating profusely during the day I focused hard on controlling my body's perspiration. I would take deep breaths in and then exhale slowly through my mouth several times to reduce my heart rate and to calm my anxiety attacks. Sometimes I would even use the colour technique and envision my body as it lay on the bed. I would visualize the sweat leaking through my pores and very, very slowly I would 'make' the movements of the droplets of sweat reduce their speed and dry up on my skin. After this I would concentrate hard enough to visualize no more drops of sweat leaving the inside of my body. Pretty soon (perhaps a half hour later) my entire body would be sweat free and cool and calm with a steady, regular heartbeat. These exercises depleted what little energy I had and so I was always exhausted physically, mentally and emotionally. At times I would slip into a light sleep only to be awakened by throbbing eyes, which I knew had to have become terribly infected, as were my ears. Even my scalp was itching uncontrollably.

Again, I would deplete my energy, using the same techniques to ease the pain and discomfort in my eyes, ears, scalp, feet, not to mention all the other cuts and bruises. Even the pain I was experiencing in my tummy from the brutal rapes was eased temporarily...I repeat temporarily. I did all that I could, not to imagine the internal physical injuries I had sustained during the entire ordeal. I imagined the worst possible things happening inside my body, growing inside of a place that was reserved only for God and my husband.

That final night the 'Keeper's' phone was ringing off the hook and I hoped and prayed that this meant that I would soon be released. Finally, he entered the room and gave me a bear hug and said that I would be going home that very night. I would be seeing my children that very day. As excited and happy as I was, I was also terrified. I was terrified of my husband's reaction to the rapes and I planned to withhold the information from him. In fact, I debated during those final hours about whether or not I should tell him or anybody else about the attacks. But I knew he would figure it out anyway.

I was horrified at the thought that this news would utterly destroy him. I was correct. Equally terrifying was the thought of seeing my two children, and I had no idea what to say to them or how to answer the million questions they were more than likely ready to throw at me. Fortunately, my mother prepared the children for the meeting and she advised them against asking any questions just yet. She told them to just hug and kiss me and be happy around me and to give me a chance to settle down for a couple of days before beginning to ask their questions.

I waited and waited until I heard the door open and close again. The 'Keeper' was back.

Lesson Learned
• The techniques I used to reduce my heart rate and ease my pain and discomfort were self-taught and took all my energy and focus to produce results during my captivity. However, after being released I was able to practice them to the point where within seconds the pain would be gone. Even now if I have a headache or any kind of pain, I can use the colour technique or visualization skill to rid myself of stray thoughts and physical pain. These techniques must be practiced frequently and mastered in order to be effective, but they can be taught if the learner is willing to seriously dedicate himself/herself to the process.

"We're born alone, we live alone, we die alone. Only through our love and friendship can we create the illusion for the moment that we're not alone."

- Orson Welles

CHAPTER 12
Released

It was very early morning, perhaps one or two a.m., on a Tuesday, that I was released. The 'Keeper' entered my room and asked me if I needed anything, to which I replied "*Yes, I need to go home*." He laughed and said that the ransom money was being dropped off even as we spoke and he had to wait on an okay call from them that all the money was, in fact, in the bag, and that there were no police following, before he could release me.

I begged him to release me somewhere close to where I could get help, like close to a hospital or gas station. He promised me that he would drop me off in a safe place, a place where nobody would find me and hurt me, a place where there would be good people around to help me call my husband. I had no idea that my husband had requested that I be given a phone to call him as soon as I was dropped off so that the police could get me to safety as quickly as possible. My husband asked the kidnapper to give him his word that he would provide me with a phone and drop me off in a safe place. Oddly enough, the 'hardened criminal' gave my husband his word and he kept it. According to the police, this was something that was unheard of in all their years of 'solving' cases of kidnapping.

We waited for what seemed beyond an eternity. Even the 'Keeper' paced the floor for hours while I tossed and turned. At one point he entered the room and undid my handcuffs saying that I could be anxious a little more comfortably without them. We actually laughed together.

He seemed just as relieved as I was that this could all be over in a matter of hours. He asked me what I would tell my husband and the children about the kidnapping.

My response was that I hadn't a clue. He apologized yet again for "*doing that to me*". He hugged me and promised to never hurt a woman like that again – ever. I believed him and I hope that he has kept true to his word.

I was extremely nervous about returning home, it was scary because I did not know what to expect or to say or how to react. In fact, I was not sure who I was or what would be expected of me from then on. I was staring into a void, a black future filled with unimaginable possibilities, not all of them positive.

In truth, I was completely unprepared for the terrible reality that was to come, for the 'real battle' would begin AFTER my release. Many people believe that being released marks the end of the ordeal, when, in fact, it was just the beginning of an uncontrolled roller coaster ride with life altering twists and turns.

Sometime into the early morning period, the 'Keeper's' phone rang. This was it, either I was going home or something had gone wrong, in which case I suspected that all patience was exhausted and I would be killed. Before the 'Keeper' answered he held my hand and said that no matter what happened, he would not let anybody kill me. There was a quick phone response of "*yes*" and that was it. It was done.

He sat down quietly on the bed next to me. The tension was thick enough to cut with a hacksaw. Suddenly he hugged me so tightly that he squeezed the breath out of me. He held my head and kissed my cheeks and head and hands and told me that I was going home at last and that he just had to wait for the vehicle to arrive. I was already free from the shackles and I began a fresh spurt of crying; this time with bittersweet joy. My 'Keeper' disappeared for a short time and left me unbound. Trying to run away at that point in time would have most likely been fatal for me, so I was patient once more.

As anxious as I was to return to my own familiar surroundings, I was equally, if not more, terrified at what would take place in the aftermath. Having endured the horrors that I did, how would I begin to explain all of this to my husband, children and parents? How would I begin to give a police report and what about the media? I prayed that everybody would just leave me alone for a little while so I could figure out how to say what had happened. No such luck.

When the 'Keeper' returned to me, he made a couple of quick phone calls outside of my earshot and I stood up from the bed, legs wobbling. It had been so long since I had actually walked, and coupled with the nervousness I felt, this caused me to almost topple over. Before I knew it he entered the room and was briskly moving stuff around; I asked if I could use the washroom once more. It made sense to do so since I had no idea where I would be dropped off, what I would encounter and how long it would take for the police to find me. He replied there was no time, once again throwing me over his shoulder like a sack of cement, then trotting through the 'apartment' and down a hill and abruptly dropping me onto the backseat of an waiting vehicle, which instantly sped off.

In the car, the 'Keeper' quickly began to loosen the duct tape from around the black mask I had been wearing for the past fourteen days and nights. He warned me to keep my eyes closed as he loosened it, and gave me instructions to stand wherever he put me, count to twenty and then take off the mask. Of course, I agreed to his terms because I did not want anything to go awry at this eleventh hour. He then placed a phone in my hand and told me that he had wiped it down and the only fingerprints 'they' would find on it would be my own. It felt familiar. He had given me back my own phone to call for help. Meanwhile the car sped at an unsafe speed around many corners and hills until it came to a smooth stop. There was no communication between the 'Keeper' in the back and the driver.

I was literally thrown out of the car and I rolled onto a drain or some other paved hollow area. I was delirious with joy and still could not believe that the ordeal was actually over; I was soon to learn that another ordeal had just begun. Dogs were barking very close to wherever I was dropped off and I was afraid of them attacking me. As it turned out, those dogs were within the confines of fenced compounds.

The car sped away, and I immediately struggled to rip the black mask off my head. There was no way I was about to count to twenty before removing it. Upon opening my eyes I tried and failed to get my bearings.

I was dizzy and though my eyes were open I could see nothing. They were terribly infected and I was all but blind. I crouched in the drain (a dry one thankfully), trying to determine how close those barking dogs might be.

Constantly rubbing my eyes gently allowed me very limited vision that was extremely blurred. I could only distinguish silhouettes. There was the blur of a nearby streetlight so I managed to get to my feet, weak as I was, and moved towards it. I fell several times during this trek which was a matter of a few feet. With my limited vision there did not seem to be any people in the area. Slowly I began to realize that I was at a street corner and that there were houses but the gates were locked. As I stood up again, and began to walk back towards where I had been dropped off I heard the faint sound of traffic speeding by. Slowly I began to move in the direction of help, or at least in the direction of people, whether good or bad.

My eyesight was gradually becoming somewhat clearer, but the stinging pain in my eyes and ears was terrible, and the pain of my feet was excruciating. I began walking on a paved surface, towards the sound of the traffic, when I suddenly remembered that I had my phone in my hand. The problem was that I could not see the numbers. I fumbled with the keypad, finally managing to call my husband's phone. Out of breath from those few steps, I slumped to the ground as a male voice answered. It was not my husband. I did not care; I just kept asking to speak to him, and then began crying again. There was no sound, and then, a familiar voice. I had indeed dialed the correct number.

I was almost incoherent, calling his name over and over again. It was a horrible mixture of relief, love and terror. He sounded as if he was almost in tears himself as he tried desperately to calm me down and to get me to focus. I suppose his many years of professional training in the aviation industry gave him the patience and presence of mind to remain calm and focused under stress. It sure came in handy at this exact moment. He asked me to try to look for anything familiar, a sign, a tree or any clue as to where I might be.

Given my limited vision I told him that I was walking towards the sound of traffic and the traffic was moving very fast. I mentioned the streetlights, a large car park and a small store. He was relaying this information to an officer on his end but everything was still very vague location wise.

I tripped and fell, dropping the phone. I sat and cried, then stood up once more and looked around, rubbing my eyes. I called my husband back. I was very close to the traffic, coming to a cross street. There was a woman jogging across the street but she did not stop to help. Why would she? I remember her looking at me from across the street with such scorn, like I was a vagrant. On the main street now, I was able to distinguish the name of a popular restaurant.

Finally, everyone knew exactly where I was, and my husband told me to sit still and wait; the police knew my location and were on their way to pick me up. I cried again and asked for the children; he said that they were fine and with my mother.

I begged to speak to my mother... oh how I begged to hear her voice, because I knew it was her prayer that God had answered.

He promised that I would talk with her soon, and that he would meet me shortly. For the first time my dear husband let his tenderness and fear show in his voice.

I crouched below a tree and hoped that nobody would see me; at least until the police arrived. I tried very hard to look at my bare feet which were in tremendous pain, but I could not distinguish my own toes. Pretty soon I heard the loud blaring of police sirens. I stood up as they pulled up in front of me...an officer approached cautiously and asked if I was Debbie Ali, to which I could only nod. Of course I had no clue at the time as to how terrible my appearance was, but judging from the looks on their faces, I must have looked like the ugliest, most smelly vagrant they had ever seen.

I managed to distinguish looks of sympathy from some, while others were too pained to do more than glance in my direction. Quickly members of the Anti-kidnapping Unit and Scotland Yard arrived, helping me into a white suit specially designed to retain any speck of material that could be used as evidence.

They all told me their names and so on; I was too busy crying and being embarrassed to care or remember. I asked for my husband and they told me that he would meet me at the hospital. Although I knew I would have to be medically examined and treated, I just wanted to go home and soak for days in tubs of warm soapy water. I was bagged, tagged and driven straight into the emergency room of the nearest hospital. While being wheeled in, the aftermath of my experience began to hit, and severe weakness and dizziness set in.

So much so that I could not focus on anything or anyone,

neither could I process any of the information and questions that I was being bombarded with. Now able to see a bit better, I looked around, desperate for a familiar face, my husband, my mother, my brother; grateful my kids could not see the terrible state I was in. There was no familiar face.

Instead, there were only strange far off voices and the sounds of people talking and relaying information at an amazing rate. There were the sounds of bags being rattled, equipment being moved around and curtains being drawn. I was still alone.

Lesson Learned
• I learned about the processes involved in obtaining evidence in such a crime. It was horrendous to say the very least.

"The fears we don't face become our limits."

- Robin Sharma

CHAPTER 13
The Reunion

At the hospital I was made to sit on a single bed behind drawn curtains as a special doctor was called in and Scotland Yard agents prepared to take verbal and physical evidence from me. As sympathetic as they were towards my situation, no one could identify with what I was enduring – nobody. A female officer from the local police force was left in the room with me and she was obviously familiar with my case details. I could tell that it was difficult for her to begin to ask me questions about the abduction, and she even admitted that she hated that part of her job. She did her duty, however, and at last asked the 'burning question'; the question I was terrified of answering; the question I knew my husband would ask and I hadn't a clue as to how I would respond. I nodded in response to the officer; yes I was raped; yes I was raped more than once.

I burst into tears again at the memory of that horrid act that can never be erased from my life, the officer cried as well and vowed to me that 'when' she found those men she would 'deal with them' as my own father or husband would. I managed a weak smile at her show of emotion and then the moment arrived; I heard my husband's voice. I panicked, my heart raced; I was overjoyed, overwhelmed, petrified and confused all at the same time. He came closer to my room and as he pulled the curtain and looked at my tattered condition, I saw such raw pain in his eyes that it haunts me even now.

He looked starved for sleep but his heart seemed to rest a bit as he laid his worn eyes on me. The bag of personal items he carried dropped to the floor, the officer disappeared and I let out a cry of relief, anguish and joy as he held on to me. I could not allow him to see my face because I was always a terrible liar and the truth would be written all over my countenance. I buried my face in my hands as he held me tightly.

He comforted me with sweet words of assurance; that everything would be okay now; that he was there now and would never leave my side again. I wonder if he was even aware of what he said, or how awful I must have smelt. I don't think he cared. I was back in the safety of my husband's arms, and for several minutes that was all that mattered, until he gently pulled away and posed the question that absolutely horrified me. The moment had arrived and I knew that I had no choice but to tell him the truth; he would have figured it out anyway. He was dazed at my positive response and he dropped to his knees in grief and disbelief. His worst nightmare had been realized and even now, years later, his grief continues. I see it, hear it and feel it every day that goes by. My crying was uncontrollable upon seeing his reaction and when he asked me how many times I was raped, he seemed to sink even lower when he saw three fingers go up.

I asked for the children and my parents and he told me that my brother and his wife (my sister-in-law) were waiting outside to see me. He had brought clean clothing and other personal items for me but I was not allowed to eat or drink anything until swabs were taken from the inside of my mouth. In fact, some of the actions that were about to be performed on my body felt almost as dehumanizing and vile as the rapes themselves, all in the name of science and evidence. The difference was that my permission was requested; and of course, I felt that I needed to allow the authorities to conduct their activities to increase the chances of catching the criminals. But it was dehumanizing.

Swabs were taken from every nook and cranny of my body, while my husband was politely put out of the room. I was glad for that because I don't think he could have handled what he would have seen. Hair samples, vaginal samples, all of my clothing; I was stripped naked on the bed with at least four people staring at my nakedness. One was a doctor, the other a female officer, the third a female Scotland Yard agent who was bagging and tagging the evidence and a fourth who was a trainee doctor carefully studying everything as the doctor poked and probed.

Humiliation hit its peak when my legs were spread and the doctor began pointing out to his trainee all the signs of rape: the bruising, the rips, the cuts and the internal injuries I sustained. I began to cry for mercy; but even in the presence of those who were supposed to seek my interest, there was no sense of mercy towards me. In hindsight, I know they had no choice but to put aside their emotions to get the job done right, but my body being put on display, treated like an example on exhibit was more than I could bear. The female officer shed tears for me and held my hand; she seemed to feel my pain. Both doctors appeared to feel nothing; perhaps because they were male.

The Scotland Yard agent tried her very best to soothe me, as a woman, by assuring me that it would all be over soon. Years later, it still is not over. Will it ever be over for me?

After all my samples were tagged and boxed for shipment, I was allowed to have something to drink and to change into clean clothing. I can only imagine how terrible I must have smelt because I had not been allowed to bathe and brush my teeth very frequently. My husband was allowed back into the room and he held on to me, refusing to let go. The doctor wrote requisitions for HIV and STD tests, as well as others for counselling.

All these events were a haze to me as my eyes and ears were badly infected. The female officer accompanied me as I was moved to another section of the hospital for tests on my eyes and ears. Unfortunately, I received an accidental blow to my badly infected left eye by a passerby. Everyone looked at me like I was an alien and murmurs spread around the hospital that I was 'that kidnapped girl'. I felt like a spectacle and I would remain a spectacle for a long time to come.

With the publication of this book I know that I will once more become a public spectacle, and once again be on the receiving end of scornful, mean, hateful and shaming reactions. However, the promise I made to my Lord and myself will carry me through this. I do this for my God and I do this for every other woman in this world, whether she has been raped, kidnapped, abused or not. This is for ALL of God's daughters.

Lessons Learned
- To an outsider the trauma is all associated with the kidnapping, but truthfully the aftermath can be just as difficult. First, there is the physical healing. Then there is a rollercoaster of emotions as a survivor deals with the demands of officialdom and their investigation, as well as dealing with friends and family, and even strangers, reacting to these experiences.

- Beyond coping with my own physical pain and mental anguish I also had to deal with the distress my husband and children had endured during those two weeks of my captivity. Even now, years later, there are still lingering consequences to being plunged so abruptly into a maelstrom of fear and uncertainty. I still catch glimpses of these consequences as we continue to get on with our lives. Their journeys were, and continue to be, very different from my own, but they are equally necessary for their healing. I thank God that He furnished me with strength I had no idea I possessed, as I grope my own way towards recovery and peace.

• My life partner and I have also struggled with our very private and individual grief's regarding the rapes. Something sacred and special was taken from us. One can NEVER regain what is lost in rape – never.

• Another of the lessons in life that I remind myself of every single day since I was abducted is that we are all born into this world with nothing and all alone, and we shall all leave this world with nothing and all alone. This is, of course, sans the spiritual lessons we may learn throughout life's journey. However, as happy as I was to be around 'people' I still felt very much isolated in my experience. This has fueled my desire to share my experiences with the world so that other women, other survivors of abuse, sexual and otherwise, can learn that they are not alone.

"In order to realize our true self we must be willing to live without being dependent upon the opinion of others."

- Bruce Lee

CHAPTER 14
The Return Home

Finally, after those final few hours of physical, mental and emotional humiliation, I was allowed to leave the hospital. Scotland Yard agents escorted us back to our own vehicle and we travelled home surrounded by several other unmarked vehicles. The media was put off and barred from surrounding my home and the hospital; but they were persistent.

As I was wheeled out of the hospital towards the waiting car by my husband two familiar faces appeared, looking anxious and relieved – my brother and his wife. I was overcome with a fresh wave of grief and love for them. I wobbled off the chair and fell into my brother's arms weeping uncontrollably.

Everyone around stared at the 'spectacle'; I cared nothing for their stares. I was with my big brother once more and that was all that mattered. Before we knew it, we formed a circle of intertwined hugs with all parties crying. They assured me that the kids were fine and that they and my mother had been caring for them during my absence. This was a huge relief to me because I knew there was nobody else who would have loved and taken such good care of them as my mother, brother and his loving wife. My children became their own and to this day the bond is incredibly strong.

I lay down on the backseat of my own car, on my husband's lap, as a Scotland Yard agent drove us home. He was very quiet and sensitive towards us and was extremely well trained. I say this because, whilst being unobtrusive and silent in our home later that day, as I spoke a little to my loved ones, he would quietly slip in a question or two. He did so in a manner that was not challenging but more like an extension of the question or answer being voiced at the time. This agent, Dave, became one of my closest and dearest friends during those first difficult days after being released, and for quite a while after. He was extremely supportive of my children and went beyond the call of duty (along with another officer) to entertain and amuse them, showering them with attention for quite a long time after my release.

He knew all the details of the case and so, as statements and discussions ensued, he was able to comfort me with his experience. As a friend, he was never once judgmental or out of line; in fact he made it a point to ensure that I never belittled myself nor allowed my self-confidence and self-worth to falter. Unfortunately, he has since returned to his homeland, and due to circumstances beyond our control, we have lost contact with each other. This will forever be one of the biggest losses of my life, and his absence will forever leave a gaping hole in my world.

When my car pulled into that same garage I had been abducted from, I smelt the familiarity of home. I sat up immediately and saw that a cousin had asked the media to leave, allowing us some privacy. I was relieved. Thankfully, there was no one at home, except for my cousin. He hugged me so tightly; and though we were never really close, I felt his relief and hurt for what he could only have imagined I had endured. He assured me that all would be well now.

Over the next few days my husband, brother and his wife, cared for me with such patience and attention that I will be forever grateful. I felt safe; especially because of the Scotland Yard agents who remained at our home for the first day or two. These agents stood on guard and alert and slept on the couches!

What truly amazed me, and still brings tears to my eyes, is the manner in which my husband put aside his own grief and cared for me that first day. He helped me upstairs, careful that I did not fall. Needless to say, I headed straight for the shower, and then my husband assisted me in undressing and taking a long, hot shower....time enough for the tub. My husband actually bathed me; he shampooed my hair, washed my body and he even dried and creamed me with soothing lotion afterwards.

I remember the rancid smell of my hair and scalp and how it refused to leave me or my pillow for nearly two weeks after being released. As terrible as the smell was, it was also familiar to me and that persistence made me feel unsettled. Unsettled in the sense that; I somehow did not belong in my real world, in my own home. There was this lingering sense that because of what had happened to me I now belonged to the dark, sinister world of the kidnappers. It was all very difficult and confusing, and it would be quite some time before I would regain my sense of self or belonging. Sometimes I still feel that I do not belong in this world or with my own family anymore.

After bathing and changing into comforting and familiar clothing I settled onto my favourite spot on the couch and for the first time in my life, my brother brought me a meal. He, his wife and my husband all had to coax me to eat....which I did, only because I knew they would feel better if I ate a little. I was not hungry; I wanted to see my babies, my parents.

They were on their way over, my two darling children; and I can only imagine how nervous they must have been, especially my son who was, still is and always will be, extremely close to me. My daughter, being so young at the time, (only 6) did not fully understand the gravity of the situation. The only thing that brought it home to her was the fact that she was no longer in her own bed, with her own blankets and toys, and her mummy was missing.

My son on the other hand, (aged 8) was older and better able to understand what a kidnapping is and basically what it meant.

I was nervous about what I should say or should not say; in the end I followed a mother's instinct.

Upon hearing their voices echo through the house, my eyes immediately filled with tears but I realized I should withhold the depth of my emotions from them, to protect them from my own pain. I tried to get up to greet them but for some reason I froze. They came to me cautiously. Here they were, my reason for living and they did not jump all over me. Instead they looked at me a bit apprehensively, almost as though they weren't quite sure that I was really their mummy. They were like puppies, making sure the scent was just right.

They both examined me and were visibly shocked by my physical condition; the dark circles under my eyes, the obvious weight I had lost, the paleness of my skin, and so much more. Fortunately, I had thought to wear long pants to hide the scrapes and bruises I had sustained.

Their questioning looks slowly turned to smiles as I covered my mouth with my hands to contain the scream I was so sure was about to escape. It did not. Instead, joyful tears streamed down as my babies put their arms around me and sat on me. I never wanted to let go, and for a while they never wanted to let go either.

Kisses were showered on their heads, cheeks, hands, tummies and every area of exposed skin! My joy was complete, I had survived to be with my two children and nothing was ever going to take them away from me again!

They innocently asked me where I had been all this time and if I was feeling okay; I could only nod that I was alright and promised to answer all of their questions the very next day.

Then my parents entered the room, bringing me bright colourful flowers to signify their joy at my return, and there were more hugs and kisses to be shared. My mother swears she never shed a tear through this whole period of time; such was her faith. She simply said that she had never doubted for a minute that I would return and that God always answers her prayers. She was correct on that count.

Just seeing her strength added to my strength, and I will maintain until the day that I die that if I could have half the strength that she possesses, then I will be a truly strong woman. It is one thing to be kidnapped and tortured, but quite another to have this crime perpetrated against your child; your flesh and blood.

I was equally happy to see my father, and very much surprised that he had survived the ordeal. Despite suffering several strokes, my father had proven his strength by refusing to give up on my return home. Although he allowed himself to cry, he also willed himself to live, and to keep calm, all the while praying for my return every single day, for hours at a time. In fact, my entire family never ceased to pray for me and I believe that their persistent badgering of God Almighty swayed Him to spare my life.

Lessons Learned

• It is said that God sends us angels to help us in our times of greatest need. The agent, Dave, was my angel, sent to keep me from sinking into a deep, dark abyss of depression, pain and loneliness. I will miss him always and I consider myself truly blessed to have known someone so remarkable.

• I am also very proud of my two children, for their ability to survive such a trauma. They endured this harsh intrusion into their lives, the confusion and uncertainty of those days, and yet they remained stable emotionally, mentally and physically.

*"You don't create your mission in life –
you detect it."*

- Viktor Frank

CHAPTER 15
The Aftermath

Myself:
The recollection of the details of my abduction and my experiences as a hostage for the purpose of police reports was very difficult; however, I knew that it was necessary. Having to relive the gory particulars of my rapes was especially terrible. I increasingly understood what the word violation means.

The next step was to determine whether or not I had contracted HIV / AIDS from my kidnappers. After all, there was no telling what kind of diseases those men were carrying around with them, or for how long. Of course, simply having to walk into the Clinic to have the tests done was in itself a painful experience. All eyes were glued on my husband and me. It was there that I realized how much concern for my welfare there was in the public domain. One or two of the nurses, and one doctor, recognized my face and name and sympathized with our situation. They even told me they had prayed for me at their churches, mosques and temples.

Going about what had been my daily routine was not the same and I found that I just could not function in the same way that I did before. Somehow, everyone looked different; the vehicles, the streets, the homes and the voices, all sounded strange to me. I figured that this was because now everything was coloured by the dark side of life that I had experienced. Even daylight held new meaning for me, and suddenly I found myself appreciating everything that life had to offer. I also found a purpose to my life, to tell my story and educate as many people as possible on the true nature of this crime called kidnapping. I also lived to care for my children and husband. It was the beginning of a whole new life for me and I was determined not to allow the kidnappers to win yet again by locking myself in my bedroom.

The sympathetic stares of my neighbours, while their concern was appreciated, soon began to anger me. I felt like an animal on display because everyone ogled me like I was a clown or some strange creature. Pretty soon I hated going out for that same reason; everyone stared. Of course, the same questions lay on the tips of everyone's tongues. I was forced to retell the story again and again. And always, there were the questions of whether I was raped or not, and how much ransom money was paid. I quickly got to the point where I bluntly told people that I did not wish to discuss the ordeal.

Ironically the people closest to me were the most reluctant to ask prying questions, yet total strangers, relatives and friends found it appropriate that I should divulge this intimate information to them. I certainly did not feel like I wanted to at the time, as I was terribly burdened with guilt.

At first I felt like I was to blame for the assaults and the kidnapping. It would be a long time before I could get past the blame and 'forgive' myself for not being more prudent on the morning of my kidnapping.

At times I am still unsure as to whether or not I have truly forgiven myself – and for what? I still do not know.

It was incredibly painful to share the gory, horrid details of the rapes with my husband, but I understood that it would have been unbearable for him not to know. He was always there whenever I awoke from a nightmare; he was there every single night. Those kinds of dreams haunted me for a long time and after years they still occur too frequently for my liking. I have received counselling from religious leaders, social workers and even a psychiatrist, but none of them could relate to my experience. Nobody could tell me what to expect of myself, my children and my husband; nobody could give me the answers I sought. I realized that I would have to figure out on my own how to come to terms with the terrible experience I had endured – alone.

The one person who came closest to pointing me in the right direction was my psychiatrist; someone whom I consider a very close friend, someone who truly cared and was non-judgmental in his approach to my ordeal. To him, I will forever be indebted for his sincerity and goodness of spirit. Our work together, and my experience with God, gave me such hope; hope that I would mentally, emotionally and physically survive the aftermath.

I found that I could not look at my reflection in the mirror because the person that looked back at me was a total stranger. I was able to brush my hair, put on my makeup and dress myself without really looking at myself.

One morning I awoke determined to look myself in the eyes. That was a somber day because I saw a battered, humiliated and shattered woman; it was unbearable. How could such nasty, degrading acts have happened to me? All that I had endured still seemed surreal to me. My worst nightmare had become a reality.

One strategy I used to cope was placing little notes to myself in the places I definitely would be - all over my bedroom, on the front of the dresser or next to my Bible. I had to learn to see myself as God sees me – pure, clean, washed and undefiled. In God's eyes, no matter what was done to me I was still his precious, beautiful Debbie, perfect in every way. In other words, I had to see myself the way I see my little daughter. I needed to relearn how to love myself, and believe me this task can be very, very daunting.

Women across the world need to see their true value and

worth. We are priceless, every single woman, regardless of how battered and bruised we are from life. We must learn to cherish ourselves before we can cherish others, or we will have no love left to give. Of course, this step came years after being released from captivity.

To me, starting to love myself meant spending just a few minutes every day doing something for me; whether it was polishing my toenails, trying on new makeup, taking a nap, exercising, talking to a friend or reading. I also took a lot of time to spend with God's word, and in prayer, giving thanks to God. This dedication served me well as it brought with it inner peace, and strength to do His bidding.

Within a few weeks I was able to begin speaking out to private and public audiences, as well as to get on with my daily life. In fact, I remember driving myself to a nearby store alone, just a few days after being released... despite much protest from my husband and children. However, I insisted because I felt I needed to prove to myself that I could move on, that I was once again in control of my life, and part of taking back my life was refusing to allow the kidnappers to control my life and movements.

Having a routine certainly helped to settle the chaos. The routine of dropping the kids off to school and attending to their matters served as a constant distraction for both my husband and me. But there was no hiding how 'famous' my name and face had become. Total strangers would walk up to me and express their sympathy, and I began to feel as though I was making a real difference for women the more that I spoke out and gave interviews. Women would admire my strength and courage and encourage me to keep going. But while I thanked them, I also told them that my strength was not my own. I was only able to do the things I did because of God's strength and my faith in the Lord.

The rapes haunted me day and night, and if anyone walked too close to me in a crowd I would break down into tears. That made shopping for the kids that Christmas very difficult but I felt that it was important for them to enjoy something of the season.

There were mornings when I could not get out of bed, and I realized that I was sinking into a deep depression. I began using medication to help me relax and sleep and this helped me a great deal. I lost count the number of times I cried at the memory of the assaults and the horrid treatment that was meted out to me.

One night in particular, I found myself rubbing my skin on the walls of the house. There was no use in taking yet another shower; I could still smell the men, the garbage and the dog. Fortunately, my husband caught me just as I began scraping my skin off while crying hysterically.

There was the overwhelming feeling of worms and maggots creeping and crawling on and beneath my skin and I just wanted them dug out and gone. That was how filthy and vile I felt; that was how worthless and violated I felt. My husband had to hold me that night, all night.

There were days that I was a complete mess, completely unable to function and when the situation got the better of me. There were also days that I could cope with the kids, and everything else, and slowly those days came more frequently than the difficult ones.

"I pray all the time that my children will never in their lifetime experience what I had experienced and went through."

I wish I could express to my husband how much I had grieved to see him, and to touch him again, and yet now it seemed so difficult.

I got to the point where I had to avoid too much contact with my children and parents because they would not have been able to deal with my disintegration. I felt overwhelmed, by the memories of the kidnapping, and now with the responsibility of protecting everyone around me from myself. If I self-destructed, then everyone else would fall apart and I knew that I had to stay strong for everyone.

Another coping mechanism I used was to allow myself a specific but limited amount of time each day to think about the ordeal of the kidnapping, to grieve and rage within myself. I began with a couple of hours each day when I would allow myself to let go and not have to protect anybody else's feelings. This time was usually at night after the kids were in bed. Gradually, over time, I reduced the time to one full hour, then half an hour, then fifteen minutes. Now, I do not permit myself to indulge in those destructive thoughts, unless I find myself in a situation where there is a clear reminder of the abduction.

By imposing these limits on myself, I was able to control the amount of negativity I allowed into my mind, body and spirit. This technique served me well as it protected my loved ones from seeing me fall apart, as well as giving me freedom to grieve.

"Pain is only bearable if we know it will end,
not if we deny it exists."
- Victor Frankl

I also worked at reconditioning my mind. By this I mean that for every terrible thought that crept up on me, I would replace it with two or more wonderful memories of my past or my time in Heaven (which I will discuss shortly). This took some doing to get the hang of, but eventually it began to help. It allowed me to focus more on joyous memories of my past and less on the negativity of my kidnapping.

Sometimes for meditation at night or early on mornings, when the children were asleep, I would dwell on the feeling of complete security I experienced in Jesus' arms while I was in Heaven. I would beckon that feeling to fill me up with every breath that I took and with each deep breath, I would feel better, stronger.

There were days I would spend a long time just looking at my body in the mirror, trying to find something about it that I still liked. There were days I found nothing likeable, and days that I loved myself. It was a troublesome learning process, and even my husband was not aware of how much pain I was in; of how much pain I still endure every day that goes by. But time does create distractions and a gradual distancing from the event, so in that sense time is a healer. Our inner selves, however, will always bear the scars of such powerful painful episodes. My experience has changed who I am, but some things have remained the same - my heart and soul.

Through further self-analysis, I realized that everything I was doing was still relative to my husband and children and I needed to clearly define who I was as an individual. This was painful, but I had to learn to accept me just the way I was, flaws and all.

Too often, even now, I allow myself to feel worthless based on what those close to me say, but I always jolt myself back to the truth, that truth being that God sees me as beautiful and untarnished and therefore I am just that. For a long time the battle raged between what I knew and what I felt, but with the help of God and my faith in Him, I have been able to allow God's truth to prevail.

I was also forced to come to terms with the fact that my husband would never again see me in the same light, and this was incredibly difficult to accept. In order to come to terms with this I needed to detach myself from him emotionally. As a woman I found it extremely difficult to find solace in myself at times; my life revolved around my family. I believe this happens because women are natural born caregivers and so, more frequently than we would like to admit, we look to our husbands and children for appreciation and validation.

"Great spirits have always encountered violent opposition from mediocre minds."
- Albert Einstein

Now I know who Debbie Ali is; I found that identity with my new purpose and in loving myself. I learnt that it is okay to be proud of myself and all of the things I have accomplished, and how to measure my development and success in terms of heavenly wealth. Now, living life is just that – living; not being bothered by all the pettiness that life and people throw at me. Now I want to experience all of the things I never did before, with new vigour.

But there was, and continues to be, a need to be accepted for who I have become (because of the kidnapping) by those I love most dearly. I suppose that means I still need to detach myself from some persons close to me, and keep my eyes glued to the tasks I must perform.

I even went through a self-destructive phase where I was acting out, as rebellious as any teenager, trying to find myself in this world. I wanted to do all of the things I knew were considered improper or forbidden; so I did. I created a master plan that even included getting a tattoo. I failed miserably, chickening out when I walked into a shop and saw the needle at work on a man's arm.

I purchased a pack of cigarettes from the supermarket, enduring questioning stares from the cashier who knew me by sight. My excuse was that the cigarettes were for someone else. That night, with my kids spending the night at my mom's, I lit my first smoke and ***, just one puff was enough. I coughed my way into the next morning and it left me with such a headache that I felt like I had a hangover. Needless to say, the rest of that pack of cigarettes was dumped in the garbage. Smoking was not for me.

Next on my list was getting drunk. Boy oh boy did I pay for this one. I got drunk under the watchful eyes of my big brother who did not approve of this adventure but indulged me. One night at his home I drank myself into a stupor and passed out. Of course, I was a laughingstock for the next couple of days. I threw up the next morning and was left with a lingering hang over for the rest of the week. Drinking (other than socially) was not for me.

The most dangerous act of rebellion on my list was to have an extramarital affair. I tried to imagine how I could arrange or even do such a nerve wrecking thing. Somehow I did not feel the excitement and danger that some say one feels! I hadn't the gall to be with someone – anyone, just for the sake of sex. I was still me, and Debbie could not do such a thing. Love had to be the key ingredient and there was love only for my husband; my heart was his alone and so having an affair was not for me either.

I have since developed a different list of things that I would like to do - ride a bicycle, learn to swim, learn to play the guitar and the piano, and to sing in public. Perhaps someday I will check them off.

"If you can dream it, you can do it."
- Walt Disney

I will say this, resuming work has been one of the best decisions I ever made. Working gave me a steady routine, financial independence and it helped me to regain my personal confidence through my abilities as a professional. I continued my studies and today I hold my Degree in Mass Communications. I stopped and started several jobs, looking for my niche, that place where I felt comfortable and I could settle for a long time.

My life is still an emotional rollercoaster ride at times, but I have the will to survive and to do God's bidding, and those are sufficient to allow me to overcome the terrors life has thrown at me.

My personal battle will continue but at least Debbie Ali survived. The real Debbie Ali, who continues to evolve and learn and grow in every aspect of life.

> *"It does not matter how slowly you go as long as you do not stop."*
> *- Confucius*

My Husband:

Having to deal with myself is one thing, but trying to understand how a man processes such a nightmare is a whole other can of worms. Men truly are from another planet! Over time I came to understand that men feel somewhat emasculated when they are not able to protect their loved one. They do not see that they are not to blame, even when the situation is out of their control, such as not even being present.

Men simply view the situation as their failure to protect those who are in their charge. A man's first impulse is to vent fury and rage like a tornado, to 'take down' whoever is responsible for causing such damage to their lives. Just about every male I spoke to said that they would want revenge at the very least, and to see the criminals brought to justice.

Neither my husband nor I have seen justice as no one has been caught in connection with my abduction for ransom. The ransom money has not been traced either. Yet everyone imagines that because I am alive and back at home with my family, that all is well.

Nothing could be further from the truth! I was amazed that when my husband was asked how he was coping, he never pretended that everything was okay. Instead, he would bluntly say that he was not handling the situation at all. Some perceived this as a cry for help, but he was simply being honest. This gave me the strength to openly say to others that I was not okay, and that I was not happy, and that I would be haunted for the rest of my life. It gave me the opportunity to vent my own anguish openly and not pretend, at least not for people outside of my immediate family.

My husband always told me and continues to, that whenever he looks at me he sees those *** raping me. The problem is he cannot erase those thoughts from his mind. I admire the strength and sense of calm under fire he showed as he handled the negotiations for my release. He did not break under the pressure. The police and Scotland Yard detectives all grew to respect him for the way he managed the situation. True, I was the hostage, but he had to keep a clear mind and steady emotions, managing his own fears and the emotional needs of our children and other members of our family. After my release he proved himself a true professional, and a man of great courage, as he continued to perform his duties at work. Nobody knew the internal battles he fought every single day, and I am sure that fight continues even today.

As a man, he has endured great difficulty in making peace with the fact that my body was defiled. He has to constantly remind himself that although my body was assaulted my mind and heart remained untarnished. As a father, he is more determined than ever to protect his children at all costs; as am I. His rules are stringent, and at times become a nuisance to me, but I force myself to remember why this is so important to him. He has lost much in this life, as have I, but hopefully given more time; he will learn how to truly live again. As a professional at work, he has demonstrated immense strength of mind through his ability to put aside his personal hurts and perform the tasks at hand.

I am certain that you, Dear Readers, will appreciate the fact that greater details of our marriage after the kidnapping cannot be revealed in this book. This is necessary to preserve some level of privacy in our lives.

My Children:
It is often said that children are smarter and far more resilient than given credit for. My son (then 8 years old) and my daughter (then 6 years old) are living proof of this. The admiration I have for my two children is tremendous because they have had to cope with all types of ridiculous stories flying around them but through it all their faith in us, their parents, never wavered.

My son, being the elder of the two, had a firmer grasp of what had taken place and that I had been severely hurt during the ordeal.

Over the weeks and months that followed he asked me questions about what was done to me during the abduction, and I would always try to answer as honestly as possible. However, if he found that I looked disturbed by his question or something on the television; my sweet son would steer away from the topic.

He became my bodyguard. Whatever part of the house or yard I was in was where he would be – to protect me from the bad men.

He was also convinced that if he had been at home the morning of my abduction, that he would have fought the men and protected me. So in a way, my young son partially blamed himself for not being there for me; thus his attempts to make it up to me by guarding my every move after that. Thankfully, after a while he grew to understand that the situation had not been within his control.

While my husband and I did all within our power to give the children some form of normalcy and routine in their lives, our lives were still very much disrupted by the events. I was forced to leave a mobile phone with my son at school so that during the school day, whenever he grew worried about my welfare, he could call me and hear my voice. If I did not show up promptly at dismissal time he would call me to ensure that all was well. This nervousness was not healthy for him. His anxiety for me also caused him to pull back on activities that did not include being under our watchful eyes whereas before the kidnapping he had been a very active child, involved in many different sporting activities.

His protectiveness of his little sister grew as well, and he spent a great deal of his time at school ensuring that she stayed where either he or a teacher could see her at all times. At times he would even accompany her to the washroom, and whenever he was unable to keep an eye on her himself, he sent one or two of his closest friends to look after her – the darlings did this ever so willingly.

One afternoon on the football field, a classmate began making jokes about his mother being stolen and bad things done to her. Needless to say, my son flew into a fit of anger when the child would not stop his taunting and a scuffle ensued. The boy was disciplined and I am proud to say that my son got the last one in; in that fight. He has had to ignore nasty stories about his father dealing in drugs and that the kidnapping was 'pay back'. He was forced to listen to stories that I had run away with a boyfriend and was blackmailing his father for money, and even that I had gone crazy and was staying at 'St. Ann's Mental Hospital.' Neither my son nor my daughter believed any of the tales. It could not have been easy to hear gossip and dirty remarks about our situation, and to have to turn a deaf ear, but my children knew the characters of their parents and knew that none of the tales were true.

My sweet son still keeps a watchful eye over me and I have seen many demonstrations of his 'fighting skills' should anyone ever try to steal me again. His grades dropped temporarily, and he would be very moody at times, both at home and at school. Thankfully, he is steadily returning to his old self and has taken refuge in his 'first love' – football.

This is his way of venting his emotions and refocusing his energy in a positive manner. My husband and I have recognized that his outlet is important for him and so we have firmly decided to allow him to continue pursuing his passion.

These days my son is not so paranoid, but he is still ever cautious, ever wary of strangers and passing vehicles. He will visually sweep an area and note details of everything around him and if there are any persons we should be wary of, all in an instant. While I am happy that he is aware and cautious, I recognize that this experience has taken away much of his childhood innocence. He is no longer the happy-go-lucky boy he once was. Since 2006, he has become a very strong, mature, protective young man. Is this fair to him? Should an innocent child lose his freedom (in many ways) because his mother fell victim to a horrid crime? I often rage about the unfairness of this, and it hurts my husband and I whenever we think about the psychological damage that has been done to our first born child.

My innocent little daughter also suffered through this. Aged six at the time of the kidnapping, she could not fully understand what was happening, however, she knew that I was not present in her life for two weeks and when I returned I looked a fright. She also knew that I cried a lot and had terrible nightmares.

She heeded her big brother's warnings of where to play and danger spots. My baby daughter, from whom I tried to keep the ills of this cruel world, came to understand firsthand the dangers that strangers posed. I will forever regret this loss of innocence. At such a tender age, she was plunged into the dark side of life and people; she is now always on the alert for 'bad people'.

Though some normalcy has returned to her life, she did suffer a great deal, emotionally and mentally. My daughter was the happiest child ever seen, always dancing, singing, laughing and playing, but after the kidnapping, for a while, she would slip in and out of character. There were times when she would drift off into dreamland and grow, very, very sad. This disturbed me terribly and still grieves my soul. So much was stolen from me, and so much from my children.

Not long after my release, my daughter's grades began to steadily decline and she grew very sad indeed. In a bid to get her back to being the happy little girl she once was, my husband and I worked continuously to distract her, keeping her as busy as possible. Our efforts paid off and she is herself once more. My baby daughter has been through a great deal emotionally but her sweetness has survived.

There were times when she would ask me questions, such as was I choked and slapped. I would always answer as honestly as possible; however, I was careful not to allow her to know how badly those memories affected me. So, she was told the truth and her questions were answered, yet she was still protected from the harsh reality of what really transpired.

I remember one particular incident when the two kids and I were waiting for their father to return to the car from using an ATM machine. We were left alone for all of three minutes, with the doors securely locked, but within that space of time, my kids dropped to the floor of the car several times in fear. Whenever a stranger walked too close to the vehicle, my son would grab hold of his little sister and command her to hide on the floor before a stranger could see them. That pained me endlessly.

For a long time they continued to respond this way to strangers in our community, and elsewhere. They lived in fear of the unknown, and of strangers. To their innocent minds, anything unknown was a threat to be avoided at all costs, however, I am indeed very proud to say that this fear has not incapacitated them. In fact, it has served to make them more aware of their surroundings than the average adult tends to be.

Another painful reminder of the irreparable damage done to my children psychologically occurred one afternoon after school. I told my daughter that I would be in a nearby classroom speaking to a teacher. After playing outside for a while she forgot where to find me. In a fit of panic she began screaming and ran straight to her brother, who, equally panicked though more controlled, began a search for me. My babies combed the entire school, my daughter in tears and my son close to tears, but trying to be strong for his baby sister. When they finally opened the right classroom door my daughter flew straight into my arms, shouting that she thought that 'they' had taken me again. My son dropped to the floor in relief and almost broke into tears also. No child should have to live like this.

I am most proud of my two blessed children, especially since their faith in God and Jesus has been further strengthened by what our family has endured. However, they have been scarred deeply and their loss of true childhood innocence will remain a terrible regret of mine.

My Family:

While I remained very close to my brother and my parents, I also found it a strain to have to protect them from the true horrors of my abduction. My brother and his wife took care of my children like their own; they made their favourite foods, took them out on trips and did everything possible to distract them. They even took time off work to help everyone deal with the terrible situation.

However, all of the pictures they took of my babies over that two-week period showed my kids looking sad and confused. Not one picture found them smiling. It still breaks my heart to look at those images. To my brother and his wife I will be forever indebted for their kindness and willingness to just take my kids and care for them.

I especially felt like I needed to protect my parents, because of their health. To do this I found that I had to keep a certain amount of distance from them, and as a result they grew even more concerned about my wellbeing. All that I could do was to continue to reassure them that I would be okay and that I just needed a bit of space to myself. Eventually they understood, but this understanding only came with time. Initially in their eagerness to help me, they crowded me. Now things are more or less back to normal between us all and the kidnapping no longer comes up in conversation. Whether they intentionally avoid it or not, I am not certain. In my heart, I feel there is no need to rehash the past, especially when it holds such pain for us all. It is important to me, however, to note that the strength my mother displayed during that ordeal was unimaginable. She remained strong for my father, my husband and most of all for my children. I will never, ever understand how she was able to accomplish this given her own pain as a mother. Just the thought of my precious daughter living through such a nightmare is enough to break me down. I know this much is true, I do not possess the strength my mother has, for if I had been in her shoes at the time, I would surely have died of grief.

Friends and Relatives:
When it came to dealing with friends and relatives I quickly grew very impatient, and at times resentful, of their presence. It seemed as if those closest to me were not prying and questioning, however, there were others who saw fit to ask the most intrusive questions.

After a period of humouring their invasion of my privacy, I began to bluntly tell everyone that I simply did not wish to discuss the kidnapping anymore and I would answer no more questions. I am certain that some thought this rude of me, but I simply did not care for their insensitivity.

There were also persons from my community who concocted wild stories about my husband and I, and we did all that we could not to lose our cool about those accusations. There were stories of me running away with a lover and blackmailing my husband for money. There were stories of me screaming uncontrollably in terror when I was released from my abductors. There were even stories that my husband was trafficking drugs and a deal went sour.

Strangely every one of these tall tales began with people who we thought knew us better than that. I was thoroughly disappointed in many individuals, and for the first time I was able to see their true colours. There was even a close female relative who only suspected that I had been raped, and yet she looked at me with such scorn and disgust that I was totally humiliated and shocked at her reaction towards me. It was obvious to me that she had been discussing my abduction and speculating on the details. How could someone I thought I knew so well, turn out to be so cold and unfeeling, especially as a woman herself.

There is nothing about anyone that can surprise me anymore – nothing.

Lessons Learned
• Surviving a prolonged, life threatening experience such as a kidnapping leaves one changed forever; in some ways for the better; in some ways not.

• It affects more than just the one person. It has an impact on their immediate family, their extended family, their closest friends, even sometimes their co-workers. Nothing about the world is the same for anyone touched by the incident.

• Knowing this, and accepting this fact is necessary in moving forward, hopefully in a positive direction.

"Be happy, but never satisfied."

- Bruce Lee

CHAPTER 16
A New Way of Life

Dealing with a kidnapping and its after-effects is overwhelming, wide ranging, complex and long lasting. Beyond the survivor there are implications for spouses, children and other close family members and friends.

Nothing can adequately prepare you for such a dire event. That said, one should still be as prepared as possible for life threatening events. Since my kidnapping, life has become a training camp, a battlefield where success might someday, unexpectedly, once again be measured by one's ability to simply survive daily life. My old ideas of realizing career dreams and obtaining true happiness are now replaced by a dreadful awareness of the ills of society and the evil that individuals are capable of. While this change is not necessarily a positive one, it has nevertheless placed me in an advantageous position, because my inner eye has now been rudely opened. For the first time I can see potential for danger all around; at times, even when the likelihood of it occurring is slim to none.

It is my opinion that, as a general rule, there has been little attempt to sensitize the general public about preventative measures in order to avoid becoming a victim of kidnapping or violent crime. Even worse, there is little done to help survivors of violent crime to cope with what has happened to them.

After my own experience I found only vague and irrelevant material on strategies for coping with my marriage, my spouse, my children, the public and most importantly, with myself.

While this recounting of my experience is very painful to me, it is my hope that someone, somewhere, reading my words will be helped or comforted in some way. If these words of advice can save one person's life, then my agony in recollection will have been more than worth it.

I also wish to stress that no one should take my suggestions and conclusions as carved in stone, to be applied in all circumstances. This book contains only the shadow of the lessons I have learned, and the assessments I have made, based on my specific experiences and the persons involved. No two situations or criminals are alike and, therefore, what worked for me may not necessarily work in another situation. However, under circumstances where your very existence is at risk, I do believe that my suggestions are worth a try.

Here are some very basic preventive and safety lifestyle considerations:

Around the Neighbourhood:
- Be aware of your neighbours' vehicles, so that you can easily recognize a suspicious one circulating in your community.
- Note workers in your community and how much attention is paid to you and your family.
- Be aware of gossiping neighbours/relatives who are capable of making public sensitive information about you or your family members, e.g. occupation, expenditures, trips abroad, alarm systems or the possession of a firearm.
- Keep your affairs private, especially your financial status.
- Always be aware of strange passers-by, vehicles etc. And their proximity to your children and loved ones.
- If possible, gather support in your community to have it gated. This will limit the ease with which deviant individuals can enter your area.
- Encourage your community to hire security patrols or form a neighbourhood watch group.

Around your vehicle:

- Try as much as possible to avoid parking your vehicle far away from where you must enter a building.
- Whenever possible park in a well-lit area or under a streetlight.
- Check around your vehicle/home before entering or exiting. Look for loitering strangers, signs of a break in, open doors, punctured tires etc.
- Check the backseat before you enter the vehicle. When you open the car door the interior light should come on giving you enough light to see the inside of your vehicle. This could save your life and will only cost you a few seconds extra.
- When approaching your vehicle, have the metal part of your longest key protruding between your index and middle fingers. This can be used as a weapon if you are attacked and can buy you a few seconds to try and escape.
- Once in your vehicle, lock all doors before you even turn on the engine.
- If using an automatic door/gate, drive your car out onto the street before shutting it. This can prevent your vehicle from being blocked in.
- When returning home and parking in your garage, keep your vehicle in reverse gear until the door/gate is closed. This will enable a quick exit if intruders enter. It also places you in a more prepared position to ram out of the way any vehicle or persons that may be attempting to enter your premises.
- When driving in traffic, ensure that windows are up, doors are locked and child safety locks are on. Also place handbags, briefcases (all valuables) out of sight (i.e. below the seat or on the floor).
- If an unknown vehicle is behind you as you approach your driveway or parked around the corner, always drive around the block until no one is following you. You can also drive to the nearest police station. ONLY enter your garage or yard when there is no other strange vehicle around. Enter quickly and close quickly. All it takes is 10-15 seconds to attack or nab you.

- Try as far as possible to drive an obscure vehicle rather than a flashy distinctive one. This is, of course, a matter of choice.
- Take a defensive driving course.
- Keep vehicle gas tanks full and vehicles in good working condition at all times, for obvious reasons.
- If possible, conduct business at locations which offer secure parking in non-isolated areas. Use online facilities to conduct business where possible. This will minimize your vulnerable moments and interaction with the public and/or criminal elements.
- One of the simplest ways to avoid being kidnapped or attacked is to vary your routes. Try as far as possible to leave your home at different times; use a variety of routes to go to work.
- Vary the days and times you visit the gym, pharmacy, supermarkets, etc. This way it is more difficult for a criminal to track your movements. Remain unpredictable and change up your routines.

Around the House:
- Place adequate, effective lighting around your home. Trim large trees that can be used to climb to windows or that throw large shadows where intruders can disguise themselves. Keep ladders safely secured.
- Colour code your keys for faster access in and out of your home or have a master key for all locks.
- Secure all possible entrances to your home with locks and alarms.
- Locate weak points or areas of vulnerability around your home and fix or compensate for them. For example, placing tall/large pieces of furniture against a ground floor window can help to deter an intruder from entering.
- If possible, and appropriate, plant defensive plants such as thorny roses, prickly raspberries or stinging nettle below potentially accessible windows where someone might try to enter your home.

- Regularly walk the perimeter of your home checking for broken windows or unexplained footprints in flower beds suggesting your home and family are being observed.
- If possible, keep a dog to alert you to the presence of strangers.
- Keep your cell phones and cordless phones charged at all times and within easy, immediate reach. This is especially important in an emergency.
- Keep alarm triggers, phones, remotes, keys etc. on your person at all times, and at your bedside at nights.
- At night keep all bedroom doors open for easy access in the event of any type of emergency.
- Place a list of important phone numbers somewhere it can be easily accessed - police, security firm, fire, alarm company, a close neighbour, current family phone numbers, names and numbers of friends of the children. These numbers can also be programmed into speed dials on phones.
- Be aware of items around the home that can be used as weapons: golf clubs, kitchen tools, fire extinguishers, heavy chains, pepper spray, aerosol sprays etc.
- Have a plan for advantageous and safe spots in your home where you can attack an intruder or secure yourself and loved ones while awaiting help.
- Take self-defence lessons. You will learn about the sensitive areas of the human body to focus on if you are attacked (i.e. throat, ears, eyes, groin or left arm or leg.)
- Use night lights and lights on timers to create the illusion that someone is in the house even when you are away. This also means that you do not need to come home to a dark house. If your lights are absent and your neighbours' lights are still on something might have happened at your home. Be alert.
- Have your house keys in hand before leaving your vehicle. Waste no time outdoors fumbling for keys. Your attacker can use these few seconds to pounce.
- Know where your smoke detectors are located because you could trigger one as an alarm against an intruder.

- Always be able to find your way out of your home, office or garage with your eyes closed. This can be easily learnt through practice and is important if you are blinded or blindfolded; you may still have a chance at escaping if you can exit very quickly.
- Keep a quantity of cash at home. Perhaps if intruders are satisfied with their loot, they may be less inclined to inflict further injury or kidnap you. This is also important in any emergency situations that may arise.
- If someone from a maintenance or utility company visits, ask for proper identification before permitting entry. If the visit is unscheduled do not hesitate to call the company's office to confirm that this person is a legitimate employee of the company.

Around the Family:
- When you are in public with young children make sure they are always within your sight and preferably within easy reach.
- Have very strict arrangements made for the picking up and dropping off of your children at school and other activities. Speak with your children about safety precautions and equip older more responsible children with a cell phone to be used in an emergency. There should be pre-set emergency numbers and children should be taught responsible usage, and have a safety plan.
- Keep sufficient cash on your person at all times for an emergency, as well as any special medication. This must be easily available to you and could save your life if you are kidnapped or in any dangerous situation.
- Keep your phone numbers private and instruct children and help not to divulge such information to anyone, nor to disclose the whereabouts of family members to anyone.
- The recorded message on the telephone should be obscure and not identify the family but should simply ask the caller to leave a message.
- Consider having your phone numbers delisted and only give your contact information to selected persons.

- Another strategy is to have a true and false password system. Family members must know these passwords so that if someone calls during an attack or kidnapping you can tell your captors that you must use your password. You can then simply use the password that indicates that all is not well and you might be sent help in the nick of time.

It is important to note that while these measures may not necessarily *save you*, they may be able to cause a delay, grant you enough time to escape or frustrate your attackers enough to move on to an easier target. Remember, criminals and kidnappers are in search of easy money! They do not want to have to work very hard for it, so if you are sufficiently prepared and frustrate their attempts to 'grab' you, they will simply move on to someone who is an easier target. If that person is equally well prepared, then obviously kidnappings will decrease in frequency and the incidence of violent crime will gradually diminish.

The key here is awareness and creating safe spaces for you and your family. Over time, these precautions will simply become a way of life. Some argue that I am now paranoid and this is no way to live. I absolutely agree, but we must also be proactive instead of reactive when it comes to crime. Statistics prove that certain kinds of crime are on the increase and it is my fervent belief that by refusing to be sitting ducks, or helpless victims, we can halt this trend and change the statistics.

"It is only when we silent the blaring sounds of our daily existence that we can finally hear the whispers of truth that life reveals to us, as it stands knocking on the doorsteps of our hearts."

- K.T. Jong

CHAPTER 17
My Visit with Jesus in Heaven

You may recall that at one point, a few days before my release, I knew that I was dying because I was simply emotionally, physically and mentally drained from trying to stay alive. I would like to share with you a little more about what happened during those hours.

Constantly using my mind to effect positive changes in my body wore me down terribly. It was this, coupled with the length of time the ongoing negotiations were taking, which made me feel like I could no longer go on. Exhaustion overcame the deep love I had for my children and husband. I surrendered to God and the result was astounding!

As aware and conscious as I am at this very moment, so too I was at the time of my death. I was fully aware of the fact that I was slowly dying and I allowed it to happen because I was exhausted. I was exhausted from trying to stay alive and sane, from trying to deny the torture I had endured. My battered and wounded body could no longer support my spirit; thus, my spirit had to leave its earthly accommodation.

Very slowly I felt all of the pain in my body begin to fade. Gradually all of the discomforts I had endured for so long began to disappear into – nothingness. They simply ceased to exist, yet I remained conscious. Not once did I forget who I was or what was happening to me, nor did I forget any of the memories of my past. I was still 'alive'; still very much Debbie Ali.

In fact, I felt better than I had ever felt in my life. I was rejuvenated, energized, mentally, emotionally and physically alert and strong.

How is this possible? This is death. Death is painless and the human spirit regains its freedom. Upon dying, I felt more freedom than I ever knew existed; free from the heaviness of my human body, free from the anguish of suffering, free of all pain. But I was also aware that I was losing my loved ones. It was the thought of never seeing my children and husband again that tempted me to feel sadness, however, I found that sadness, hurt and emotional pain were impossible for me to feel. In the heavenly realm the only emotions that exist are love, peace, bliss, contentment and endless joy. I actually tried to feel sadness and regret at having to leave my two babies behind but I simply could not.

I realized I was hovering over my physical body. I saw myself lying on the mattress exactly the way I was positioned; handcuffed and curled up on my right side. I was shocked to realize that I was looking at myself. I tried to comprehend how I could have been looking at myself when I still *was* myself. Upon closer inspection I realized that my chest was not moving and, therefore, I had to be dead.

Perhaps a normal reaction would have been horror and panic. My reaction was simply "I'm dead, oh damn." I simply could not feel the terror, fear, shock or sadness that one would expect in such a situation. At no time did I feel less like myself nor did I forget anything in my life. I remained fully conscious and aware throughout my entire experience. While some may be skeptical I ask only that you, Dear Reader, finish this book and ask yourself, "What if all of this really is true? Will I deserve to live in the presence of Almighty God or in this blissful realm, wherever it is?"

What follows is a description of my experience in heaven. You are welcome to your personal interpretation and opinion, of course, but as far as I am concerned, it all happened; it was all real and was NO DREAM.

VISITING HEAVEN

Before I could fully assimilate what was happening to me, I sensed a very real presence behind me. As I turned around, not feeling any fear, the most brilliant white light I had ever seen began to appear before me. I turned back to look for my body but I could no longer see it. As I spun around again, I faced THE most astounding sight I have ever beheld. The white light was so bright now that if I was in my body again, I would have been unable to look at it. Yet, despite all of its brilliance, I looked directly into that light without squinting. I looked at the light completely unafraid, indeed with complete peace and bliss. Profound joy resounded within my entire body. There are simply no words in any language to describe the indescribable, except of course in the language of the angels.

Out of the brilliant white light stepped Jesus Christ. From this point onwards, he spoke to me without using words. By this I mean that there was some form of telepathic communication between us; we spoke through thoughts only. I knew he WAS the Lord, and I was overwhelmed with joy and excitement; so much so that I fell to the ground before His feet. I dared not look up at his face to see if he looked like the pictures I grew up with. Instead, what I saw was a silhouette of his form; a human figure with so much white light radiating from Him that it was impossible to distinguish specific features such as a face or clothing. All that I recognized was white light emanating from a form that I just knew was Jesus Christ. He had a distinct voice (though I heard it in my mind); it was very, very soft and gentle. It exuded love, grace, peace and forgiveness.

I asked the Lord if I was dead but he never responded to this question. He simply touched my head; it was the softest touch I have ever felt, softer even than my daughter's hand at birth; and with this touch there was a feeling of deep warmth that spread throughout my being.

Still prostrated before Him, I could distinguish what seemed to be a pair of golden sandals but when I looked closer I realized that actually **My Lord was barefoot too!**

He lifted me up to stand before Him and the only emotion I was able to feel in His presence was love, joy, peace and everything positive. I believe it is impossible to feel anything else in Heaven, especially in the presence of God.

Jesus said,
"Child your suffering is over.
There is no more pain, no more sorrow, no more tears.
You are tired and you can rest now."

He smiled and my heart lit up. I did not see His facial expression or His actual smile but somehow I knew that He was smiling and He was happy that I was home again. Before I realized what was happening, he scooped me up into His arms like I was a newborn baby. He held me so tenderly, folding me into His bosom, and just as a baby automatically curls up in his mother's arms, so too I curled up snugly into the arms of my Lord. I slept in absolute comfort.

When I awoke, I was still in Jesus' arms but this time we were on a beach. Like a newborn infant, totally new to the things of this world, I was totally new to the things of Heaven. It was the most awesome sight. The colours and smells were unlike anything that any artist in this human world could illustrate. The air was crisp and clean and there was a gentle breeze blowing; just enough to wisp my hair slightly. It would be months before I remembered the feel of this wind and the gentle sound it made in Heaven. This gentle blowing sound was the breath of God which blows continuously across the Heavens. Everything in Heaven is given life by the everlasting breath of God; thus there is no need for the 'science of nature' in His realm. I once made feeble, novice attempts to paint a picture of what I saw in Heaven, but there is no blue that is blue enough for the ocean I saw. There is no colour bright enough to represent the endless white, golden light of God and Jesus. There are no words or hues that can compare to the colour of the sand that Jesus walked on. There is simply no capacity in this world to capture the colours of Heaven. It was as if everything I was familiar with in this world got a trillion times richer, more brilliant and more defined.

I propped myself upright so that I could look over Jesus' shoulder at the wonders around me – just like a restless little baby. There was the deep rich hue of blue in the ocean and a distinct line on the horizon. The water did not move; not even a little ripple, yet there was life in the ocean; aquatic life. I came to understand that the waters, trees, everything had to stand still in the presence of Jesus Christ.

It was as though the 'elements' ceased their normal activities to pay homage to the King as He was passing by. I stared in awe of the sight. The water was so still it stood in a dead straight line on the sand. The sand I looked down upon shone like crystals and reflected the white, golden light of God. The grains of sand glimmered like gems spread out before the Lord. As I looked behind Jesus' shoulder I noticed that there were no footprints left on the sand and Jesus, who knew what I was wondering, replied,

"There are no footprints because you are not supposed to go back. There ought to be no turning back."

I actually tried to feel sad at the notion of never going back to my family, and thoughts of my two children circled my head. Try as I might, I was unable to feel any sadness or regret; only joy in knowing that I would now remain in the presence of God and that all of my loved ones would soon meet me there. I began to understand God's concept of time, there is none. Even time cannot restrict God's presence; He simply – is. I dare say that on earth we rely on time to guide us, partly because life here on earth is boring and dull, a mere shadow when compared to the many wonders of Heaven. I could have stood and marveled endlessly at every single crystal of sand and still I would have continued to find wonder in every grain; so great and marvelous is the Kingdom that awaits us. So overwhelmed was I with the beauty before me that all I wanted to do was to continue my exploration of my new home and never look back. Still thoughts of my family lingered.

Jesus deposited me on the sand, but like a child I was very reluctant to let Him go. I begged Him to continue to carry me because I did not feel strong enough to stand on my own. As it turned out, I was strong enough. Often times we whine and complain to God that he has given us too much to bear and that we do not possess the strength to complete our tasks, and yet God really does know when we are strong enough to stand on our own and carry our own crosses, when we need a rest and when He needs to carry us. Like children, we need to exercise our muscles and strengthen them in the Lord in order to continue to grow and develop. It is, however, very comforting to know that He will always be there to pick us up and carry us whenever we are too weak to go on.

Because of this important lesson, I no longer live my life in worry or fear, but instead with a solid belief in the presence and love of God. We commonly refer to this belief as 'FAITH' but really I think that we often misuse the word.

Faith is not just belief that something that is not will be; faith KNOWS that what is not will be. It is an unshakable certainty, not mere tradition or habit. Thus I have converted from a 'worry wart' to someone totally free of the cares and concerns I once had. This does, in fact, make it difficult to get along with others at times because more often than not, people cannot relate to this freedom because they are so caught up in the mindset of this material world. I have seen what awaits us in the Heavens and nothing on this earth holds any real appeal to me; nothing on this earth will last forever, but everything in Heaven will last until the end of time.

To use a common expression comparing Heaven and earth is like comparing chalk and cheese, a yellow crayon to the sun, the beauty of a shadow to its true figure; like placing a toy next to the real thing.

When I stood on that crystal sand and I felt it between my toes, it was not hard on my feet although the grains of sand were actual crystal gems. In fact, the sand felt soft and grainy, yet firm. I began to feel a sensation of marvelous freedom when my feet hit the sand. I was no longer tired or weak or burdened; instead I felt better than I had ever felt before.

As I stood on the sand I noticed the plush green trees along the side of me, like we were at the end of the shoreline. The green of those trees was deeper, greener and richer than any plant I had ever laid my eyes on. It was as though each tiny leaf shone with the glitter of God and radiated with His love and joy. I turned to Jesus, who never stopped smiling, and asked about my children, to which he replied,

"Why do you want to go back, Child?
There will be no more suffering for you here.
Your children will be fine.
Do you not trust me to take care of them for you?
Would I not love them like you do?"

I had no response for Him other than to agree and surrender my argument. I realized that regardless of what troubles my children would have to endure, that Jesus would see them through it, and carry them the same way he did me. I realized that I did have enough trust in the Lord to really let go of my children, and my husband. Letting go and simply trusting God to take care of everything, to surrender control of my life, was exhilarating. The feeling was like having a truck lifted off my head. Suddenly I felt even lighter; almost floating in glee; as if I hadn't a care in the world.

As I began to let go of my family ties, God the Father appeared behind the light of Jesus. The light was the same golden white hue, only so much more brilliant. Yet still I could look at the light and my eyes did not hurt a bit. It was impossible to discern any figure in the midst of that light....because that was all there was – light. Jesus remained there next to me but God spoke to me in the softest whisper I have ever heard. His voice was the source of all life, light, beauty, love and grace that existed in Heaven. Even now I hear His voice and it is always the same whisper, which is how I know it is Him speaking to me and nobody else. Before I could even react to His presence he spoke audibly to me, but the message he conveyed to my mind was:

"My voice is a whisper to those who belong to me.
But to those who do not belong to me,
it is the worst sound they will ever hear."

To me this meant that to a 'wicked' person or someone who does not do right by God, His voice would not be a whisper but a loud, thunderous sound that would rattle the Heavens and the earth with words of judgment. He continued to speak to me and I dared not glance in His direction again, instead, I kept my head bowed in His presence.

"Child, why do you want to go back to earth?"

I told my Heavenly Father that I wanted to take care of my babies. There was no sadness in my voice or spirit when saying those words but the pull back to earth was still there, I suppose. My Heavenly Father replied,

"Child, if I allow you to return to earth you must promise to continue to do my work in the world."

I readily agreed to do whatever The Lord required of me. To this day, I still feel regret at times. In terrible moments, I regret that I desired to come back to this world when I could have stayed in the indescribable presence of God and suffered no more. But I did promise to do His bidding and this book is a direct result of his request and my willingness to help others who suffer similarly.

"Debbie, you must dedicate a book telling of your experiences here with me. I want the world to know that Heaven is as real as everything you see here.
I want you to travel the world and spread this message about my Kingdom so that my people will have courage and have hope in me.
I want you Debbie to name this book "Bare Feet" and the cover will look like this....(God showed me the cover of the book). You are not to take this book to your agent or anybody else until I direct you.
Do not worry about how the words will come or how you will speak. I, the God of Israel, Abraham, Moses and Jacob, will write for you and speak for you.
You will find the words and you will find the means. Do not concern yourself with how the book will reach its destinations; I will make a way clear for you. It is done."

Again, before I could ask any further questions, the light of God dissolved into the background and what remained was the brilliant light of Jesus. His smile was radiating now. Jesus placed His hand upon my head and blessed me. To this day, I firmly believe that when He blessed me He removed all sickness and disease from my body so that I would be whole enough to do God's bidding on earth. A tingly, warm feeling spread throughout my body again, but it was warmer than his first touch. Then he spoke,

"All will be well now, Child. Do not be afraid, nothing can hurt you again."

Oh how I longed to latch on to my Lord and never let go, but he gently released me after an embrace. Whenever I feel overwhelmed with the distractions and pain of this world, I relive my experience in His arms and the total peace I felt there; then I can continue on my journey. I wanted to ask so many questions but I was not given the opportunity, as Jesus took two steps away from me and faded into the Heavens.

In His place were Saints I knew from the Bible. Abraham, Moses and Jacob were standing on my left side and to my right were Elijah and Isaac and Mother Mary. Literally "on" my left shoulder was St. Michael the Archangel and on my right shoulder was St. Gabriel, God's messenger. Strangely, though I was not able to distinguish any features of these beings, I somehow knew the names of the ones present with me. They were all pleased; again, I somehow knew this although I could not see any of them smiling or hear them saying anything to me.... that is, all except Mother Mary.

She slanted her head to get my attention and smiled the warmest smile that a mother can share. Her gaze was comforting to me, and her eyes were a rich brown. I have a clear picture in my mind of her facial features and The Lord sent me on a hunt (some months after my release) to find an accurate picture of her. I've seen countless depictions of

Mother Mary and I even searched the Internet for a possible likeness of her beauty, warmth, love and grace. There was none to be found.

Then one day, just when I was about to call off the search, I walked into a store purely by accident. I was passing a few minutes until an appointment and simply found myself in a shop at a mall. There it was, a large painting of Mother Mary, an exact likeness of who I saw in Heaven. There was an instant familiarity of the painting's eyes and facial profile. No one has any idea who the artist is, but he/she must have been spiritually guided, because it is, to my recollection, a true depiction of Mother Mary. Needless to say, I purchased it immediately and it sits facing my bed; her warmth and love radiating through her eyes. Mother Mary smiled warmly at me and spoke these words directly to me. Words that she wanted me to include in my messages,

"God always answers the prayer of a mother."

In that instant I knew that God had answered my own mother's prayers. My earthly mother, a woman of enormous strength and character, had been praying tirelessly for my safe release, and God's heart was swayed into answering her prayer. I firmly believe that next to God's love is a mother's love. A mother's love for her children is instinctive and unconditional (at least in most cases) and therefore it is akin to God's heart. I also firmly believe that Mother Mary heeds the prayers of every mother on this earth and pleads their cases for them. God Almighty knows and understands the depth of love that a mother has for her children and responds to the sincerity and purity of their intentions and heart. Mothers of this world ought to take up the mantle that is rightfully theirs and so use the power that God has placed in their hearts and on their lips. I also believe that God is using women to stand up for Him in this world, especially in these times of deep, deep trouble. He is rising up women, with hearts for Him, to do His work here on earth; perhaps this is the reason that only Mother Mary spoke to me in Heaven.... Perhaps.

My journey back to my body was swift indeed. The Saints guided me back across the beach and for some reason, try as I might, I simply could not look back over my shoulder. I was accompanied by the Saints all the way to the beginning of the beach where I again grew very tired, the first sign of any weakness since I left my body. This was an indication that I was on my way back to my body. I sat on the soft crystal sand and I remember whispering to my new friends that I needed a rest. As I lay down on the sand, I instinctively curled into the fetal position, while the Saints and angels sat in a circle around me praying.

Before I fell asleep I remember the angels communicating with me telepathically to remind me of their presence. St. Gabriel said that he would speak to me whenever I needed guidance or help. St. Michael, however, said that he had been placed in charge of my safety until my work here on earth was completed. He will remain at my left always. I fell into a deep sleep carrying that thought. Perhaps because this was my last thought before the sleep, I did not remember it clearly....that is until I was reminded of his presence on my left shoulder by another woman of God.

When I awoke from my deep slumber, I gasped for breath and was once again in my own body. I distinctly remember how painful that first gulp of air was, because all of my physical, mental and emotional pain returned. I had returned to my body and all the anguish it held; that is, the horrible first breath into this world. My state of consciousness continued back into my body and I could recall all of the details of my trip to Heaven and back.

I was, however, no longer worried about what would happen to me. After all I was just granted another life, this time with a clearly defined purpose. I knew what I had to do; to help as many people as possible, not just because I believed that God gave me this assignment, but because I am a proactive individual by nature and was determined to have something positive come of this horror of horrors. The fear of death no longer held me under its feet and I was now truly FREE. I was certain that a resolution would be reached soon and that I would be released from captivity. As it turns out, I was correct.

Lessons Learned

• Death and near death experiences can be quite controversial. However, if you examine the vast number of NDEs across the world, where people speaking different languages, having different cultures and beliefs, all have the same or very similar experiences, I seriously doubt that it is all coincidence.

• Most people fear death, but as I have learned, it is nothing except a transition into another form; your true form, without the burden of this meat package we're currently stuck in. I never realized how heavy and ridiculous the human body is until I left it behind and felt lighter than a feather, with freedom to move at the speed of thought, faster than the speed of light and sound. That is true freedom; where nothing exists but time, space and energy; an experience that is beyond words. I anxiously await my death as I know what and where it will bring me.

*"Nothing is impossible,
the word itself says 'I'm possible'."*

- Audrey Hepburn

CHAPTER 18
In Conclusion

You might be wondering why the title chosen for my book was "Bare Feet". Our feet are vitally important to our wellbeing. The English language is filled with references to our feet; standing on our own two feet, standing strong, these boots are made for walking, walking about away from trouble, pulling yourself up by your bootstraps. These are just a few common references.

Why are bare feet so important? As a parent admires and relishes the exquisite softness, newness of smell and the fragility of a new-born baby's feet, so does our Heavenly Father. In the same way that our children remain our precious babies regardless of their ages, Our Father will forever remember our tiny, pure feet before they became tarnished with the vile horrors of this world. He will forever see the purity, innocence and vulnerability in us, His children. We will remain His innocent children forever, for whom He will give anything to protect from the evils of this world. He gave all that he could to save us from pain and anguish; He gave us His only son, Jesus Christ, who was sacrificed because of our Father's love for us. How then can we ever doubt what we are worth to Him? How then can we look at ourselves in the mirror and see anything but beauty, love and forgiveness? How many times do our own earthly children hurt and disobey us, and yet we, as parents, will always be willing to give them another chance; always love them no matter what?

My Heavenly Father, Our Heavenly Father, loves us far more than even we as parents can begin to comprehend. We enter into this cruel world 'bare' and we will leave this world 'bare'. We came with nothing, and we will all leave with nothing, save the heavenly treasures that we may or may not have stored for ourselves. The mighty hand of God forever holds our 'baby feet' in his palms, to keep us safe, to keep us strong, and to carry us when we can no longer go on.

My feet entered this life untouched; innocent to the cruelty that exists and the terribly painful paths I was forced to walk. By this I mean both spiritually and literally. I was abducted bare footed, held in bare feet for fourteen days and nights and released bare footed. Yet, my God was able to carry me through and bring me out of that furnace. Only the love of God can perform such healing miracles. Now, my feet are a hundred times stronger than December 5th, 2006.

Now, my feet can stand up to the rigors of this harsh and unkind world. My God lifted, and carried me through the ordeal and saved what life was left in me because He knew that I would need it to finish the work that He started in my life even as a mere child.

``Bare Feet`` also because we are most comfortable when our feet are unfettered by shoes. We feel the most freedom and the least inhibitions when we can run freely at the beach, in our homes and gardens. When our feet are bare it is a symbol of freedom. The irony of it all is that I was barefoot, seemingly free, yet my freedom was forcibly taken from me.

Now I understand that though I was in captivity, I was still free; I was free from the evil that pervades the hearts and minds of people. I was free because Jesus set me free. I was free because through My Lord, I was able to teach a hardened criminal about the love of God and His son Jesus Christ. I was free because I knew where I would be going when I died, and I was free because I was unafraid to die.

This is why Jesus was sacrificed, to free all of mankind from the last stronghold that the 'evil one' has on us – the fear of death, and death itself. But we can only be unafraid of death if God is in our hearts. Then and only then will we have conquered death and any stronghold that 'the evil one' may think he still has in this world. Praise God for His Son; thank you Jesus for your painstaking sacrifice just to save the human race, which your Father loved, and continues to love so very much. Thank you for saving me, a simple, humble speck of dust who loves you with all her heart and soul and mind; and ALWAYS WILL.

The Woman of God

A few weeks after I returned to earth I met a spiritual woman, purely by chance. This woman of God looked at me and asked if I ever noticed that my left shoulder was warmer than my right, in fact it had been since I was released. I had noticed but thought that the warmth was because of some injury I had sustained. She laughed and said that it was the spot where St. Michael's foot rested to protect me.

She asked me if I had ever heard his wings go up and his sword drawn when there was danger near. Of course I said *"No"*, but soon after I began 'listening' with spiritual ears for his wings and sword, but with no success.

It was only after, possibly an entire year, following my release, that I heard him for the first time, and in a much unexpected fashion. Now, I hear him whenever there is trouble brewing around me. I had been spending a lot of time in prayer and studying God's word when it happened. I was out running errands and I heard what sounded like giant wings flap into the air, creating a gust of wind. Somehow, I knew that it was him and I had an uneasy feeling that danger was about. Sure enough, a few minutes later a known drug addict entered the same store with a long stick in hand; he was in a stupor and clearly a danger to himself and those around. Because I was aware of the danger, I positioned myself to flee if I needed to.

The police were called but he ran out quickly and in a frenzied state. Before he ran off, however, he glanced at me and then pulled back, looking first at me then high above me; it was then that he ran. A minute later I heard the large wings descend calmly. I swear that when the drug addict looked at me, he seemed to recognize something and it scared him away. This was not to be the last instance of these miraculous warnings of danger. I have heard and felt St. Michael's presence at my side many, many times over the years and I firmly believe that he has protected my loved ones and I from impending calamity.

The Language of Angels

Mere words in any human language cannot adequately describe the wonder that is Heaven: the sights, sounds, smells and feelings of that realm. It can only be experienced.

Since my kidnapping I have visited many churches and listened to many different versions of people claiming to be filled with the Holy Spirit and "Speaking in Tongues", and while I refuse to judge anyone anywhere on their claims, I dare say that what I witnessed and heard with my own two ears was, in fact, the language of the angels and thus an authentic experience of what is commonly known as 'Speaking in Tongues'. Very little of what I have heard comes close to my experience in Heaven.

Oddly enough, one day my little daughter began humming similar rhythms, totally oblivious of the fact that she was singing the songs of the angels in Heaven. At play one afternoon, while she hummed her little innocent song, I asked her where she had heard the tune. Of course initially I thought that she may have heard it at school, on television or on the radio. She just 'made it up; she said; she had not heard it anywhere. To me that was further confirmation from God that what I heard was, and IS, real and that it is only with the innocence of a child that one can perceive the reality that is Heaven. This is my perspective.

As joyous and relieved as I was that my kidnapping was 'finished' the experience also brought me a new resolve; a determination to relive those terrible events as many times as needed, in the interest of making the public aware of the crime that is called kidnapping. This resolution started with the horrors I endured but I eventually understood that the lessons to be learnt from my experience ran far deeper than the crime itself.

Indeed, there were many more harsh realities my husband and I were to face; realities that we were not prepared for. I have tried to share those realities within this book. The truth is that nobody can prepare you to face such unfair treatment and even in the 'developed' and 'civilized' countries, there are very few trained professionals who are properly equipped to address the mental, emotional and spiritual issues that arise after violent crime.

In closing I ask that you share the contents of this book with everyone you know. I ask this not for my fame and fortune but for the spreading of God's word and the message that he wants all of mankind to know. I humbly ask that you remember my final words:

"Call me crazy; I care not; for I know to whom I answer,
and where my final destination lies. Heaven exists.
It is as real as the tea I am drinking, as real as the air I am
breathing and as real as I am sitting behind my computer.
I am living, breathing proof that God is real and
His Kingdom is real. I am living proof that He saves.
I firmly believe that I am His proof to the world that
He sees all, He hears all, He knows all that is done
in the darkness and in the light, and He saves."
Repent and be saved. God bless you all.

PSALM 91

Whoever dwells in the shelter of the Most High
will rest in the shadow of the Almighty.
I will say of the LORD,
"He is my refuge and my fortress,
my God, in whom I trust."
Surely he will save you
from the fowler's snare
and from the deadly pestilence.
He will cover you with his feathers,
and under his wings you will find refuge;
his faithfulness will be your shield and rampart.
You will not fear the terror of night,
nor the arrow that flies by day,
nor the pestilence that stalks in the darkness,
nor the plague that destroys at midday.
A thousand may fall at your side,
ten thousand at your right hand,
but it will not come near you.
You will only observe with your eyes
and see the punishment of the wicked.
If you say, "The LORD is my refuge,"
and you make the Most High your dwelling,
no harm will overtake you,
no disaster will come near your tent.
For he will command his angels concerning you
to guard you in all your ways;
they will lift you up in their hands,
so that you will not strike your foot against a stone.
You will tread on the lion and the cobra;
you will trample the great lion and the serpent.
"Because he loves me," says the LORD,
"I will rescue him;
I will protect him, for he acknowledges my name.
He will call on me, and I will answer him;

I will be with him in trouble,
I will deliver him and honour him.
With long life I will satisfy him
and show him my salvation."

AMEN.

Printed in the USA
CPSIA information can be obtained
at www.ICGtesting.com
LVHW020042040524
779162LV00003B/560